THE BBC TV SHAKESPEARE
Literary Consultant: John Wilders

RICHARD II

THE BBC TV SHAKESPEARE

AS YOU LIKE IT
HENRY VIII
JULIUS CAESAR
MEASURE FOR MEASURE
RICHARD II
ROMEO AND JULIET

THE BBC TV SHAKESPEARE

Literary Consultant: John Wilders
Fellow of Worcester College, Oxford

Richard II

MAYFLOWER BOOKS, INC.,
575 LEXINGTON AVENUE,
NEW YORK CITY 10022.

Published in the United States by Mayflower Books Inc., New
York City 10022.

Originally published in England by The British Broadcasting
Corporation, 35 Marylebone High Street, London W1M 4AA,
England.

The text of *Richard II* used in this volume is the Alexander text,
edited by the late Professor Peter Alexander and chosen by the
BBC as the basis for its television production, and is reprinted
by arrangement with William Collins Sons and Company Ltd.
The complete Alexander text is published in one volume by
William Collins Sons and Company Ltd under the title *The
Alexander Text of the Complete Works of William Shakespeare*.

Library of Congress Cataloging in Publication Data

Shakespeare, William, 1564–1616.
  Richard II.

  (His The BBC Shakespeare)
  1. Richard II, King of England, 1367–1400 – Drama.
  I. Wilders, John. II. Title. III. Series: Shakespeare, William,
  1564–1616. Selected works. 1978
  PR2821.A23 1978   822.3'3   78–24130

ISBN 0–8317–7396–0

Manufactured in England

First American Edition

*PR
2821
.A23
1978
Jan. 1999*

CONTENTS

PREFACE

Cedric Messina

The plays of William Shakespeare have been performed not only in theatres, but also in country houses, inns and courtyards, and one of the earliest references to performances was made by William Keeting, a Naval Commander who kept a journal of a voyage to the East Indies in 1607. The entry for 5 September, off the coast of Sierra Leone, refers to a performance of *Hamlet*, and that of 30 September to a performance of *Richard II*, both being staged for Portuguese visitors aboard the East India Company's ship *Dragon*. And so the plays started their triumphant progress of performances throughout the civilised world.

BBC Television is not inexperienced in the presentation of Shakespeare's plays, and indeed as early as 1937, on the first regular television service in the world, it presented a full-length version of *Julius Caesar*. Since then, thirty of the plays have been presented, the more popular ones many times over. Some have been produced in encapsulated form like *An Age of Kings*; some done on location like *Hamlet* at Elsinore with Christopher Plummer as the Prince and Robert Shaw as Claudius, and *Twelfth Night* at Castle Howard in Yorkshire with Janet Suzman leading the cast as Viola. Studio productions have included *The Tragedy of King Lear*, and *The Merchant of Venice* with Maggie Smith as a memorable Portia. Many productions have been taken from the theatre and translated into television terms like the Royal Shakespeare Company's *The Wars of the Roses* and The National Theatre Zeffirelli production of *Much Ado About Nothing*.

In the discharging of its many duties as a Public Broadcasting Service the BBC has presented during the last ten years at peak viewing time on BBC 1, on every fourth Sunday night, *Play of the Month*, a series of classical productions ranging from all the major plays of Chekhov to a number of Shavian masterpieces. Aeschylus has been produced in the series, and so have many of the plays of William Shakespeare. So not only in the presentation of Shakespeare, but also in the translation to the screen of the great dramatic statements of all ages and countries, has the BBC demonstrated that it is fully equipped to meet the enormous challenge of *The BBC Television Shakespeare*.

The autumn of 1975 gave birth to the idea of recording the complete canon of the thirty-seven plays of the national play-wright. (Thirty-six of the plays were published in the First Folio of 1623, exactly half of which had never been published before. The thirty-seventh is *Pericles, Prince of Tyre*, first published in the Quarto of 1609.) The first memo on the subject of televising all the plays emanated from my office on 3 November 1975, and was addressed to Alasdair Milne, then Director of Programmes, and now Managing Director, Television. We were asking for his blessing on the project. His reply was immediate and enthusiastic, as was that of the present Director-General, Ian Trethowan. This warm response to the idea stimulated us in the Plays Department to explore the possibility of making the plan a reality – six plays per year for six years, with one odd man out. It has been called the greatest project the BBC has ever undertaken.

There followed a succession of meetings, conferences, discussions and logistical quotations from engineers, designers, costume designers, make-up artists, financial advisers, educational authorities, university dons and musicians. The Literary Consultant, Dr John Wilders, was appointed, as was David Lloyd-Jones as Music Adviser. Alan Shallcross was made responsible for the preparation of the texts. On the island of Ischia, off the coast of Italy, Sir William Walton composed the opening fanfare for the title music for the series. Visits were made to the United States of America to finalise coproduction deals, decisions were taken about the length of the presentations to average about two and a half hours per play, and more seriously, the order of their transmission. This was a game played by many interested parties, some suggesting they be presented chronologically, which would have meant the series opening with the comparatively unknown *Henry VI Parts 1, 2 and 3*. This idea was hastily abandoned. A judicious mixture of comedy, tragedy and history seemed the best answer to the problem. It was decided that the English histories, from *Richard II* through all the *Henry IVs, V* and *VIs* to *Richard III* would be presented in chronological order, so that some day in the not too distant future, the eight plays that form this sequence will be able to be seen in their historical order, a unique record of the chronicled history of that time. The plays that form the first sequence will be *Romeo and Juliet*, *Richard II*, *As You Like It*, *Julius Caesar*, *Measure for Measure* and *Henry VIII*.

The guiding principle behind *The BBC Television Shakespeare* is to make the plays, in permanent form, accessible to audiences throughout the world, and to bring to these many millions the sheer delight and excitement of seeing them in performance – in many cases, for the first time. For students, these productions will offer a wonderful opportunity to study the plays performed by some of the greatest classical actors of our time. But it is a primary intention that the plays are offered as entertainment, to be made as vividly alive as it is possible for the production teams to make them. They are not intended to be museum-like examples of past productions. It is this new commitment, for six plays of Shakespeare per year for six years, that makes the project unique.

In the thirty-seven plays there are a thousand speaking parts, and they demand the most experienced of actors and the most excellent of directors to bring them to life. In the field of directors we are very fortunate, for many of the brilliant practitioners in this series of plays have had wide experience in the classics, both on television and in the theatre. The directors are responsible for the interpretations we shall see, but as the series progresses it will be fascinating to see how many of the actors take these magnificent parts and make them their own.

It was decided to publish the plays, using the Peter Alexander edition, the same text as used in the production of the plays, and one very widely used in the academic world. But these texts with their theatrical divisions into scenes and acts are supplemented with their television equivalents. In other words we are also publishing the television scripts on which the production was based. There are colour and black and white photographs of the production, a general introduction to the play by Dr John Wilders and an article by Henry Fenwick which includes interviews with the actors, directors, designers and costume designers, giving their reactions to the special problems their contributions encountered in the transfer of the plays to the screen. The volumes include a newly-compiled glossary and a complete cast list of the performers, including the names of the technicians, costume designers and scenic designers responsible for the play.

The title page of the First Quarto of *Richard II*, published in 1597, reads

The Tragedie of King Richard the second.
As it hath beene publikely acted by
the right Honourable the Lorde Chamberlaine
his Servants.

There were four subsequent Quartos, and the play was published in the First Folio in 1623. The scene of King Richard's deposition was not published until the Fourth Quarto of 1608, after the death of Queen Elizabeth I, who saw parallels between herself and Richard and was strongly opposed to the scene being played on the stage during her lifetime. The play has 2757 lines, 287 of which have been cut, as is shown in the text. *Richard II* is the eleventh play in the accepted chronology of the thirty-seven, and this production was recorded in the Television Centre, White City, London, in April 1978. On 6 February 1601, a performance of *Richard II* was arranged for the following day by friends of the Earl of Essex, as inspiration for his ill-starred revolt. After its failure, Essex was imprisoned, condemned to death, and executed on 25 February.

In this production, Derek Jacobi, who plays King Richard, is surrounded by a splendid company including many of the leading names in our classical drama. As old John of Gaunt, Sir John Gielgud, one of the most acclaimed Richards of his younger days, plays opposite one of the most acclaimed young actors of our day. The Duke and Duchess of York, two of the most important characters, are portrayed by Charles Gray and Dame Wendy Hiller. Dame Wendy is one of the great actresses of the English Theatre, and portrayed Eliza Doolittle in the first film of Shaw's *Pygmalion* to be made. She has appeared in many classical roles both at the National Theatre and at the Old Vic. Charles Gray is one of the leading character actors of the English stage and has an impressive role-call of classical plays in which he has performed – from Tyrone Guthrie's production of *The Alchemist* to *The Merchant of Venice* on television.

INTRODUCTION TO RICHARD II

John Wilders

Shakespeare was profoundly conscious of the effects on the personal lives of Englishmen of the fall, deposition and death of Richard II. He not only devoted a whole play to this subject but he referred to it repeatedly and at length in six other plays, the two parts of *Henry IV*, *Henry V* and the three parts of *Henry VI*, in which he portrayed the reigns of Richard's successors. The consequences of the King's dethronement, as Shakespeare saw them, were prolonged and terrible, for it removed from the seat of power a monarch who had ruled the country by a hereditary right which had been unbroken since the twelfth century and, as a result, left the throne open to be fought over by rival claimants in the Wars of the Roses, a series of civil struggles which ended only with the accession of Henry VII more than eighty years after Richard's death (see the Genealogical Table on page 18). The moment at which the King removes the crown from his own head and hands it to Bolingbroke is, therefore, one which, in Shakespeare's eyes, radically altered the course of English history.

It was, presumably, for this reason that Shakespeare chose to make the transfer of power – the deposition – into the central, pivotal scene of his play. Everything that occurs before this episode leads up to it and everything that happens afterwards follows as a consequence of it. Shakespeare uses the first three acts of *Richard II* as a preparation for this event and, just before it arrives, he warns us, through the words of the Bishop of Carlisle, of the bloody effects of the act we are about to witness:

> Let me prophesy –
> The blood of English shall manure the ground,
> And future ages groan for this foul act;
> Peace shall go sleep with Turks and infidels,
> And in this seat of peace tumultuous wars

Shall kin with kin and kind with kind confound;
Disorder, horror, fear, and mutiny,
Shall here inhabit, and this land be call'd
The field of Golgotha and dead men's skulls.

Then, as Richard hands over the symbols of his power to the usurper, he enumerates them in order that we may linger on this moment and grasp the weighty meaning of the process we are witnessing:

I give this heavy weight from off my head,
And this unwieldy sceptre from my hand,
The pride of kingly sway from out my heart;
With mine own tears I wash away my balm,
With mine own hands I give away my crown,
With mine own tongue deny my sacred state,
With mine own breath release all duteous oaths;
All pomp and majesty I do forswear.

Like several other episodes in this play, the deposition has the measured, deliberate quality of a ritual.

Richard II is, however, more than a very moving, solemn portrayal of a king's downfall: it is also an analysis of the reasons why this downfall occurred. The causes of great political crises are usually complex and originate from the pressure of circumstances which have accumulated over a period of years. Modern historians repeatedly try afresh to trace to their ultimate roots the causes of the Civil War or of the First World War, and Shakespeare is in this play acting in part as a historian, tracing the deposition back to its origins, which are shown to be various and at times obscure. We know that he undertook what was, for him, considerable research before he wrote this play and that he took the trouble to read the accounts of Richard's reign given by earlier historians, poets and dramatists. Some of these accounts were biased against the King, portraying him as a degenerate, incompetent spendthrift from whose government the country was providentially saved by Bolingbroke. Others were hostile to the usurper, showing him to have murdered a saintly monarch in order to satisfy his own arrogance and ambition. Shakespeare takes a more disinterested, balanced attitude, placing the responsibility for the deposition partly on Richard's incompetence and unpopularity, partly on Bolingbroke's firmness and talent for winning support, partly on mere chance, and partly on the unique relationship between the two characters. As a result, he induces us to watch the steady succession of events in such a way that we give our entire sympathy neither to the monarch nor the usurper. Moreover, this combination of circumstances, all working in the same direction, is so powerful that the catastrophe seems inevitable: the two men seem to be engaged in a process of which neither is wholly in control.

The earliest of the events which sets the drama in motion, the murder of Thomas of Woodstock, Duke of Gloucester, has occurred before the play opens, and the responsibility for this crime is the subject of the feud between Bolingbroke and Mowbray with which the first scene begins. Under the presiding judgement of the King, each accuses the other of plotting Gloucester's death. The man actually responsible for the murder is Richard himself, but Shakespeare does no more than hint at his guilt at this stage, perhaps in order that the central character should not lose our sympathy immediately, and perhaps so that we should perceive the difference between the show of secure impartiality which Richard displays in the first scene and his inner, secret guilt which is not revealed until the second scene. This contrast or separation between the authoritative public figure and the fallible private individual is one which is made frequently throughout the play.

When Bolingbroke and Mowbray insist on settling their quarrel by formal combat, Richard first postpones their encounter and later, when it is about to begin, suddenly intervenes and sends both men into exile. This is the second step in the process which results in the King's downfall.

So far, though we have heard of Richard's degeneracy and guilt, we have not actually seen him commit any objectionable or unlawful act. On the contrary, his decision to banish Mowbray and Bolingbroke is apparently taken for the admirable motive of preventing civil strife or, as he puts it,

> For that our kingdom's earth should not be soil'd
> With that dear blood which it hath fostered.

Ironically, his decision produces the very calamity it is designed to avoid. The next step he takes is, however, unlawful and politically inept: he seizes for his own purposes the wealth and property which the absent Bolingbroke should rightfully inherit on the death of his father, John of Gaunt. In so doing he defies the very laws of succession and inheritance by which he himself occupies the throne. As York protests:

> Is not Gaunt dead? and doth not Hereford live?
> Was not Gaunt just? and is not Harry true?
> Did not the one deserve to have an heir?
> Is not his heir a well-deserving son?
> Take Hereford's rights away, and take from Time
> His charters and his customary rights;
> Let not tomorrow then ensue today;
> Be not thyself – for how art thou a king
> But by fair sequence and succession?

Moreover, the King's seizure of Bolingbroke's possessions has disastrous political consequences, for it provides the latter with a pretext for returning from banishment and demanding his rights. It is at this point, too, that we hear in fuller detail of Richard's incompetence and unpopularity: he is a prey to irresponsible flatterers; he has lost his people's support by heavy taxation; he has wasted his wealth on personal extravagance. With Richard's popularity thus low in the eyes both of his subjects and the audience, Bolingbroke takes the momentous step of defying his king and returning to England.

What precisely were the motives for his return Shakespeare never openly reveals. In contrast to Richard, who pours out his most intimate feelings spontaneously, Bolingbroke keeps his inner self concealed. There is no scene (and Shakespeare could, obviously, have written one had he chosen to do so) where Bolingbroke is shown in the actual process of deciding to return, no soliloquy in which he displays his motives. When he meets first his uncle, York, and later the King, he insists that he requires no more than is his due as his father's heir. Yet, though he returns apparently to claim an inheritance, he actually gains a kingdom. Shakespeare has omitted the evidence on the strength of which we should either condemn or applaud him.

In addition, while Richard has lost the support of his subjects, Bolingbroke is very adept at winning it. Even as he passes into exile, we are told, he 'dives' into the people's hearts and, on his return, he ingratiates himself with his most powerful allies with promises of reward after he has succeeded:

> I count myself in nothing else so happy
> As in a soul rememb'ring my good friends;
> And as my fortune ripens with thy love,
> It shall be still thy true love's recompense.

Whereas Richard showed his rashness by taking Bolingbroke's inheritance while the latter was in exile, Bolingbroke shows his shrewdness by choosing deliberately to land at Ravenspurgh when Richard is in Ireland, for when the King returns he finds that virtually the whole country has defected and that he is already a defeated man. By sheer misfortune his only remaining loyal soldiers, the Welsh, have disbanded a day before his arrival. He now has nothing with which to defend himself but his right to rule and the strength of his character, and when he faces his opponent at Flint Castle, even these powers fail him.

Bolingbroke declares that he has come only for what is his due:

My gracious lord, I come but for mine own.

Richard, however, crumbles before Bolingbroke's presence and at once hands over his person and his kingdom:

Your own is yours, and I am yours, and all.

He has himself completed the process of his own downfall. His deposition is now inevitable and follows almost immediately.

Shakespeare allows the causes of this bloodless revolution to unfold and accumulate gradually. As an analysis of political change *Richard II* is subtle, lucid and even does justice to those hidden motives which must always perplex the historian. The shift of power, however, serves only as a background to the figure of Richard himself, who dominates the play and whose personality and reactions to events are Shakespeare's chief interest. To begin with he is shown to be outwardly self-confident but inwardly corrupt and hence has the legal but not the moral right to govern. These two facets of his character are conveyed to us by Shakespeare's alternation of scenes of public ceremony, in which the monarch appears in the pomp of his authority (I i; I iii), and private scenes where his callousness and degeneracy are either discussed in secret or exposed by his own unguarded talk with his intimates. For example, Shakespeare first shows us Richard's callous, flippant reaction to the news of Gaunt's sickness –

Now put it, God, in the physician's mind
To help him to his grave immediately!

– before he shows us the prophetic, dying man himself. These impressions reflect unfavourably on Richard and we soon hear Gaunt's impassioned and wistful eulogy of an England which has become corrupted from within by Richard's irresponsibility. During these first two acts Shakespeare has gradually and deliberately lowered the King in the estimation of the audience.

We see no more of Richard until his return from Ireland when, deprived of that power which allowed him to control the lives and property of other men at his whim, he sees himself for the first time as vulnerable, essentially no different from his subjects:

> I live with bread like you, feel want,
> Taste grief, need friends; subjected thus,
> How can you say to me I am a king?

From this scene onwards Shakespeare induces us to see him with increasing sympathy. What Richard loses in terms of power and adulation he gains in terms of insight into his own condition. Yet, having been transformed by circumstances from a king to a beggar, he is, nevertheless, capable of learning only a limited amount from experience. He continually fluctuates between an illusion of himself as a person uniquely privileged whose enemies will evaporate before the wrath of God, and the spectacle of himself as a martyr whose agony deserves our compassion. He has, from the start, been swayed by moods, unstable, and now he alternates between pathetic bravado and shrinking self-pity. Deprived of the only identity he has ever possessed, that of a king, it is doubtful whether he ever reaches a stable point at which he can recognise and accept his own nature. His final extended soliloquy in prison is an attempt to build a personality from the ruin of his former self, but he can find permanent satisfaction neither in the memory of what he was nor in the realisation of what he has become, and he looks forward with relief to the peace of non-existence:

> Whate'er I be,
> Nor I, nor any man that but man is,
> With nothing shall be pleas'd till he be eas'd
> With being nothing.

Together with the decline and death of Richard, moreover, Shakespeare portrays the disintegration of a family and the end of a period of history. Nearly all the major characters are blood relations, the descendants of Edward III, the father of Gaunt and York and the grandfather of Richard and Bolingbroke. The memory of Edward's authoritative, dedicated, Christian leadership is repeatedly recalled as an ideal by which Richard's weakness and egotism are measured. As the play opens, Edward's seven sons are all either dead or ageing and, with the murder of Thomas of Woodstock, only Gaunt and York remain. It is these two who recall the lost golden age and complain that Richard has betrayed the land entrusted to him. The sense of decline is seldom absent from this play. Characters are frequently shown in the process of leave-taking: the Duchess of Gloucester says a last farewell to Gaunt, Gaunt to his son, Bolingbroke and Mowbray to their homeland as they go into exile, Richard to his queen as he goes to prison. *Richard II* is full of *la poésie du départ*, 'the poetry of farewells'. The sense of disintegration is also conveyed by descriptions of decay, fading light and the autumnal season:

> The setting sun, and music at the close,
> As the last taste of sweets, is sweetest last,
> Writ in remembrance more than things long past.

> The bay trees in our country are all wither'd
> And meteors fright the fixed stars of heaven.

These descriptions of natural and seasonal decay are accompanied by stage pictures in which Richard is shown to be literally sinking, partly because this shows his natural tendency to capitulate when challenged by Bolingbroke, partly to convey to the audience the impression of his political and inner decline. When, for example, he learns, on his arrival from Ireland, that his people have deserted him, his spontaneous reaction is to cry,

> For God's sake let us sit upon the ground
> And tell sad stories of the death of kings,

as though defeated by the very news of his opponent's strength. Again, at Flint Castle, he literally descends from the battlements to deliver himself up to Bolingbroke. Shakespeare uses the visual resources of drama as well as the resources of dialogue.

As the King and his land decline, Bolingbroke self-assuredly conducts his ascent. Yet ironically he discovers, as Richard has warned him, that to gain power is merely to gain care and, though Richard is defeated, we are left with the impression that Bolingbroke has not triumphed, or rather that he has suffered a defeat of a different kind. No sooner has he come to power than he is faced with the task of making peace between his peers in a scene (IV i) of accusations and counter-challenges which recall Richard's predicament at the start of the play. Our last glimpse of him is of a man remorseful for Richard's murder, undertaking with little pleasure the responsibilities of government. When he appears at the very beginning of Shakespeare's next historical play, *Henry IV Part 1*, we recognise at once the price he has had to pay for his success:

So shaken as we are, so wan with care.

Events are, by then, already moving towards the next crisis and it is the now weary, anxious, guilt-ridden Bolingbroke who must deal with it in a very different kind of England.

Shakespeare began his career as a dramatist by writing four plays on the subject of English history, the three parts of *Henry VI* and *Richard III*. *Richard II* was probably composed in 1595, some two years after these had been completed. It differs from them in its reduction of plot and stage action to a minimum and its concentration, instead, on the relationships and feelings of the characters, particularly those of the King who dominates the play to such an extent that it may be regarded both as an account of the final years of his reign – a history play – and as his personal tragedy. Shakespeare's procedure dramatically is to place Richard in a critical situation – his return from Ireland, his meeting with Bolingbroke at Flint Castle, his deposition and his imprisonment – and to allow him fully and imaginatively to express his emotions. *Richard II*, like the plays which immediately preceded and followed it, *Love's Labour's Lost* and *Romeo and Juliet*, is written in a deliberately mannered, artificial style so that the listener is conscious of the way in which a character speaks as well as of the sense his words convey. This formal style, in which phrase is balanced against phrase within a sentence and metaphors are developed at elaborate length, is appropriate as an expression of Richard's self-consciousness, whether in his role as a king or as a common subject. Moreover, this elaborate manner of speech, combined with the formal, ritualistic construction of many of the scenes, such as the opening challenges and the deposition, may help to convey the impression of the long-established, hierarchical society of medieval England, now in its final years of decline. The varied style of the history plays portraying the reign of Richard's successor, Henry IV, reflects the life of a society which has become fragmented.

GENEALOGICAL TABLE

This is a simplified table, showing the succession from Edward III to Henry VIII and those characters who are important in *Richard II*. The dates refer to lives and not to reigns.

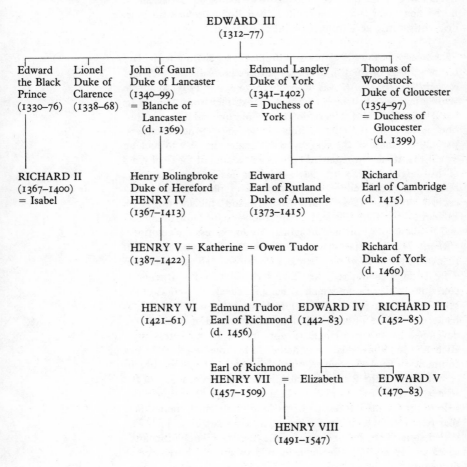

EDWARD III
(1312–77)

Edward
the Black
Prince
(1330–76)

Lionel
Duke of
Clarence
(1338–68)

John of Gaunt
Duke of Lancaster
(1340–99)
= Blanche of
Lancaster
(d. 1369)

Edmund Langley
Duke of York
(1341–1402)
= Duchess of
York

Thomas of
Woodstock
Duke of Gloucester
(1354–97)
= Duchess of
Gloucester
(d. 1399)

RICHARD II
(1367–1400)
= Isabel

Henry Bolingbroke
Duke of Hereford
HENRY IV
(1367–1413)

Edward
Earl of Rutland
Duke of Aumerle
(1373–1415)

Richard
Earl of Cambridge
(d. 1415)

HENRY V = Katherine = Owen Tudor
(1387–1422)

Richard
Duke of York
(d. 1460)

HENRY VI
(1421–61)

Edmund Tudor
Earl of Richmond
(d. 1456)

EDWARD IV
(1442–83)

RICHARD III
(1452–85)

Earl of Richmond
HENRY VII   =   Elizabeth
(1457–1509)

EDWARD V
(1470–83)

HENRY VIII
(1491–1547)

THE PRODUCTION

Henry Fenwick

Chronologically, *Richard II* can be said to open the cycle of Shakespeare's history plays; *King John* and *Henry VIII* stand apart from that cycle on either side, anomalies outside the path traced from the overthrow of the last of the Plantagenets (*Richard II*) to the crowning of the first Tudor (*Richard III*). But it was not the chronology alone that made producer Cedric Messina place it in the first season of his Shakespeare plays for the BBC. It is also in some ways an easy television introduction to the histories, both for the audience and the producer. 'It lends itself to television,' he says. 'It's not like the *Henrys*, an epic about England. There aren't any battles: all the confrontations are eyeball to eyeball.' At 2½ hours long it was also one of the shorter histories, requiring very little editing for the television screen. A happy combination of qualities for a first season.

David Giles, who had worked with Messina on the outside broadcast of *Twelfth Night*, was chosen to direct: not only an accomplished Shakespearian stage director but also a television director whose track record (which includes *The Forsyte Saga*) showed him, as Messina points out, to be adept at dealing with English history and the English character. But the first problem facing Giles was one of style, and that had to be worked out with his designers. 'You can stylise Shakespeare right down to black drapes and lighting,' says set designer Tony Abbott, 'or you can make it realistic. These Shakespeare productions are going to be reaching a very wide range of audience, some of whom won't know the plays at all. They certainly won't be all a sophisticated theatre audience. We've also got to mix studio productions with outside broadcasts. [In the first year *As You Like It* and *Henry VIII* will be performed as outside broadcasts while the other four productions will be in the studio.] That means that the studio productions must be able to go alongside the ultra-realism of the location productions. Any form of extreme stylisation was just not on. We finally went for what might be described as a stylised realism.'

The technique Abbott finally decided on for the settings was one he adopted both for *Richard II* and *Julius Caesar*, which he also designed. For maximum flexibility, cheapness, and a thrifty use of space, he decided to build all the sets from moderately large units, which could be used again and again, juxtaposed differently with each other to form new shapes, perspectives and designs, rather like an enormous Leggo set. 'What was wanted for *Richard* was an impression of big Gothic medieval architecture. I created units based on Gothic elements and by redressing those units I was able to create Windsor Castle, Pomfret Castle. I went to see Westminster Hall and saw the hammer beams and I looked at Windsor Castle, but what you are trying to create is an environment rather than a specific place: as long as you give an impression in the background that this is Westminster Hall, that is all that is needed.'

Some of the action in the play also posed problems of style for the television screen. Though, to both director's and producer's relief, there are no battle scenes ('a problem that remains to be met,' says Giles broodingly), nevertheless there are elements in the action which require simplification and stylisation: parleys, marches, confrontations on castle walls, a trial by tournament. 'It has hideous things for television,' Giles acknowledges. 'The list scene was an absolute swine. You can't do it realistically in a television studio and yet we didn't want it to get too stylised: that's why we used real horses. If we had gone too stylised with the list scene we would have had to stylise the play all the way through, and stylisation on television is very difficult. In the theatre as soon as the curtain goes up one gets the total picture: if it's a stylised picture then that's it. On television where what you see is a real head against a bit of stylised background you can only stylise if you design it shot by shot. There certainly wasn't the time for that here and I'm not sure I'd have wanted to do that anyway. The way we've done it, it obviously isn't real but I hope that you accept it. It's a terribly difficult balance to attain.'

The style problems for the costumes were of a different sort. In all the histories the aim is to be historically accurate to the period in which the play is set, but the danger of Richard's court, from the director's point of view, was that the clothes of the king and his courtiers were in real life unprecedentedly elegant. 'I desperately didn't want it to look like *The Book of Hours* – I wanted the clothes to look as much like clothes as possible. Robin [Fraser-Paye, the costume designer] said to me, "But they're extraordinary clothes." I said, "Yes, I know they're extraordinary clothes and I do know that Richard spent £2000 on one suit (which was quite a fortune then) but I want them to look real – everyday clothes that the audience can accept."'

It was a difficulty for Robin Fraser-Paye: 'After all,' he points out, 'it was a very rich court, the most decadent court up to that time. Richard was the first English king to be conscious of fashion: not only did he spend £2000 on one suit, he also invented the handkerchief. It had to be historically real, but not too pretty.' The way out of the dilemma, he decided, was to keep the colour palette down: 'I kept it to browns and burnt oranges and golds and blacks. Where a blue was used it was a blue going towards grey. Really I was trying to take the colour out. I showed the fashion consciousness with the king's favourites, Bushy, Bagot and Green – though certain quite accurate details I didn't use. The absurder of the fashions, like the very long and pointed shoes, would have been too expensive, would have got in the actors' way and wouldn't show much on television anyway. The women weren't fashion-conscious – they were more interested in showing their wealth; so I gave the Duchesses of Gloucester and York lots of fur and jewels. Queen Isabel's head-dress I took from a statue that was actually of the king's first wife, Anne of Bohemia – there are more records of her than of Isabel, who was very young. Richard's crown was authentic to the period – a slightly simplified version of Anne's crown.

'At that time people didn't wear clothes as expressions of themselves, they wore them as marks of status and class, so the designer doesn't have the freedom to do with clothes what you can do at later periods. There was no way to give individual characters to the people through their clothes – except for the king, of course, by definition. Instead I went for the power of the court, the politics of the play – again using furs and jewellery and, though silhouettes aren't desperately useful on television – they are much more useful on stage – I nevertheless went for big, powerful silhouettes for the lords.'

The historical background to the play posed difficulties for both Giles and Derek Jacobi, as Richard. Before the action of the play begins the Duke of Gloucester, the king's uncle, has been murdered. Mowbray and Bolingbroke each accuse the other, while

John of Gaunt remains discreet in public but in private blames the king:

> . . . correction lyeth in those hands
> Which made the fault. . . .

'This is a difficulty for any modern audience,' says Giles, 'not only a television audience: the first third of the play depends on a circumstance which isn't fully explained in the play and which was close to the Elizabethan audience – the murder of Gloucester. To them it was the beginning of the Wars of the Roses and a long period of civil strife. I'm sure, because most people didn't read and so much information was word of mouth, that people knew the important things in history in a kind of way that we don't, deluged with trivia as we are. For a modern audience which doesn't know the background to the opening of the play you have to take a lot on trust. You have to accept that in the first scene there's more going on than meets the eye. Even if you don't know exactly what is lurking in Richard's past, if we play it right then you will know that there's *something* there.'

The undercurrents of the first scene go at least ten years back, when the king and his first queen were humiliated, his friends destroyed, by an alliance of five lords opposing the king. 'One he has executed, one is in the tower, Gloucester has just been murdered, and now of the five only Mowbray and Bolingbroke, the two youngest, are left. Derek and I both agreed that the key section for Richard is the opening section of the play – the first three scenes. He said, "Why is he so angry in the first scene?" and I said, "He isn't – it's just high tension because it is the moment he has been waiting for so long."'

The opening posed special problems for the actor playing Richard. As Derek Jacobi explains: 'Since the first three scenes all contain allusions to the death of Gloucester, which happened before the play started, it was very necessary to find out about that and to decide exactly who was responsible for his murder. Shakespeare hasn't really given any indication from Richard's point of view that he actually saw that the murder was done. If you're playing Richard you have to decide "Did I do it or didn't I?" and inform the lines from there. The first scene is frightfully difficult – it's so sketchy for Richard. He doesn't say very much and what he says is frightfully kingly and public, but the man's got a lot to hide and a lot to lose and a lot to gain from the situation, and it's completely understated by Shakespeare.'

'In some ways it's easier on television,' adds the director, 'because by focusing on Richard in crucial moments in the first scene, and by using a major actress like Mary Morris as the Duchess of Gloucester in a part that's usually skimped over on stage, the audience does gather something of what has happened and you do realise that Shakespeare is on about something. In that way television helps. Mary said she'd never done anything that made her so nervous – five speeches to make her point and then that's it!'

Television also helped unfold other parts of the play that can pass unnoticed on stage: conspiracies open out to the voyeuristic camera with a clarity impossible in an auditorium, small scenes scurried over in the flow of the action benefit from being shot on separate sets, in more intimate detail than time or budget could allow in the theatre. 'I did notice,' says Sir John Gielgud, who is in a position to know, 'that in the little scenes that can be rather ineffective on the stage, like the scene between the three men after the death of Gaunt [Lords North, Willoughby and Ross, II i] by having just heads very close together it can be played very fast and with a very intimate feeling. On stage it seems very anticlimactic and apt to go for nothing. The fact that you can suddenly close in the stage so tightly is very valuable.'

Flint Castle also benefits enormously from being on television, thinks David Giles. In Act III scene iii Richard, in one of the most famous scenes of the play, appears on the walls of Flint Castle, first to parley with his mutinous cousin and soon-to-be-usurper Bolingbroke, later to come down from the walls and submit. 'On stage Richard has got to be way up at the back of the stage yet he has one of his most private speeches up there. It's just wonderful to be able to put the camera in close-up on to him for:

A little little grave, an obscure grave.

I personally think the camera is very helpful in Richard's soliloquy at the end of the play as well: it's all about time passing and by using mixes during the speech I think we move it on in time. I don't think we've broken the rhythm: each section of the soliloquy has him in a slightly different place doing something else, so time passes and we just swing the mixes through. It pushes you through a long period of time. When we got that idea Derek just immediately fell for it and so did I – it's just lovely to do.'

23

Most striking of all is the way television casting is able to open up hitherto neglected portions of the play. Not only is the tiny part of the Duchess of Gloucester played by Mary Morris, but the Duchess of York, often cut from the play in stage performances, is played by Dame Wendy Hiller. This, coupled with the casting of Charles Gray as the Duke of York, brings alive a whole sub-plot. 'I think if you go straight from the deposition scene to the prison scene, as is often done, you lose a great deal,' says Giles. 'If you keep the York scenes you put this marvellous period between Richard's final scenes, you enrich the Duke of York and you put a fascinating sidelight on Bolingbroke. After all, it should be a wonderful moment for him when his uncle, the last son of Edward III, kneels to him with his wife – that means he's really arrived. But they are all so busy with their own emotions that he can't enjoy it – they behave as though he's the king but they also behave as though he's their nephew and that ruins it. It makes everybody very human.'

Dame Wendy herself tells delightedly of Sir John Gielgud's comments. Sir John, well known as a kindly and encouraging man, as well as obviously an extremely knowledgeable one, has also acquired a reputation in the theatre for phrasing his remarks in a way that can sound extremely double-edged to the paranoid or unwary. 'We were rehearsing,' she recalls, 'and I had just been tearing a passion to tatters, clutching and screaming, and we came off and Sir John said: "Well, it takes an experienced actress to play it that way. Of course we always used to cut it out."' She beams, obviously delighted to have her own addition to the collection of Gielgudiana.

The part of the play that most comes alive in television, thinks Giles, is the role of the Duke of York. Not usually cast with a star on stage, since it's not a part of obvious appeal, Giles considers it 'the lynch-pin of the play – it's the audience part, the one you most easily identify with. He interprets what is happening for you, he makes our mistakes.' Similar in some ways to Polonius, Giles thinks it's actually a better part than that: 'It's brilliantly written and comes into its own on television, because you can get someone like Charles [Gray] to play it.'

But *Richard II* stands or falls by its Richard. It is not simply a historical play: as Messina points out, it is also a great lyric play, very ritualistic, very poetic. It is also, perhaps more importantly, in Messina's words 'the tragedy of one man'. To a modern audience the history fades in significance beside the complex, neurotic quality of this strikingly modern figure. 'I wanted from the first to get Derek Jacobi,' says Messina. 'I believe he is one of the great Richards and it is a performance that is completely realised in television terms.' Jacobi, then still in mid-triumph for his television Claudius and his stage Hamlet, may seem like an obvious choice now, seeing his performance. It is clearly a major piece of work. Yet he had never played the part on stage, though playing it on radio in *Vivat Rex* had whetted his appetite for the role. With him cast, the next step was to woo Sir John Gielgud, himself one of the great Richards in his youth, to play John of Gaunt – a challenging colleague for Jacobi to work alongside. There are pitfalls in Richard, as Gielgud points out. The play is famous for its verse but, says this crowned head of verse-speaking, 'the verse is very ornamented and there are too many speeches of the same kind. It can become monotonous.' 'Every line in it is amazingly beautiful,' agrees Jacobi. 'I think that's where the actor has to be careful playing it. Because you can't go through the entire play saying "Oh gosh, this is beautiful, isn't it? Oh, this is wonderful stuff." It is, but you've really got to avoid that and forget it.'

Adding to that danger, he points out, are the extra problems of working on television: 'Down, down I come' – the speech at Flint Castle – was begun on one set, interrupted, then finished on another set. 'The freedom that you get on stage when the juices are really flowing, you don't get on television. There are too many technical things to worry about – the sound, the camera.' Moreover the sequence of the scenes for shooting imposed strains: 'In the theatre Shakespeare gave you time off, little breaks before your crescendos. Here we were doing the big scenes one after another. The orchestration of an actor's tempo is thrown out of gear – but it always is with television.'

On the other hand television makes it possible to take a scene in a much lower key than is feasible in an auditorium: the camera will catch it. And a performance can be improved by the director in the editing. As we talk, none of these parts looks as though it fully makes up to him for the reassurance of a live audience and I stress how much better than good I thought he was. He smiles: 'Good! Well, that's David Giles for you.'

'I didn't do a great deal of background research. I read history at university so I already knew quite a lot about the period and about

Richard. I don't think it's absolutely necessary to do much research – what you're doing is the play and from the actor's point of view you don't need a great deal of background. It was necessary to know who the seven sons of Edward were, who succeeded whom and the relationships – and of course you need to know about the death of Gloucester!' But he already knew the play quite well, not only from *Vivat Rex* but even before: 'I was lucky, it was part of my schooldays too. It was one of my set books, so I knew about the play very well, and I found a lot of the words came back. I found it quite easy to learn.'

It was the theatricality, the play-acting of the part that Jacobi first concentrated on: 'There's an almost Chekhovian self-diagnosis all the time, play-acting – he cries wolf quite a bit and the problem comes in knowing when it's for real and where for effect, knowing where the actor in Richard stops and the man begins: the line is often very tenuous. In the deposition scene, for instance, the man is obviously at rock bottom but he gives a marvellous account of himself. The actor's instinct there is obviously: "If I've got to go I'm going to go in style." That I found fascinating. At the same time all the emotions are absolutely real for him – but he can switch it on.' He laughs admiringly. 'It's one of the easiest of the histories to follow. It really is the classic tragedy of the great man falling, of riches to rags. He starts as the great sun, the godlike king, and he ends as this poor prisoner in Pomfret Castle, all alone. A man who had the world at his feet, a court of sycophants, and ultimately played his cards all wrong.'

'There's a most wonderful line at the end of the play,' adds Messina. 'We have seen the fall of this king, seen the screw of fate turning, then in comes Exton, the man who has killed him, with his body, and says to Bolingbroke:

> Herein all breathless lies
> The mightiest of thy greatest enemies,
> Richard of Bordeaux, by me hither brought.

Throughout the play he has been addressed by every regal title. Here after his death he's called, quite simply, Richard of Bordeaux. That's a most wonderful moment!'

THE BBC TV CAST
AND PRODUCTION TEAM

The cast for the BBC television production was as follows:

KING RICHARD	Derek Jacobi
JOHN OF GAUNT	John Gielgud
HENRY BOLINGBROKE	Jon Finch
DUCHESS OF YORK	Wendy Hiller
DUKE OF YORK	Charles Gray
DUCHESS OF GLOUCESTER	Mary Morris
DUKE OF NORTHUMBERLAND	David Swift
BISHOP OF CARLISLE	Clifford Rose
DUKE OF AUMERLE	Charles Keating
THOMAS MOWBRAY	Richard Owens
QUEEN	Janet Maw
DUKE OF SURREY	Jeffrey Holland
HENRY PERCY	Jeremy Bulloch
BUSHY	Robin Sachs
BAGOT	Damien Thomas
GREEN	Alan Dalton
LORD ROSS	David Dodimead
LORD WILLOUGHBY	John Flint
EARL BERKELEY	Carl Oatley
SIR STEPHEN SCROOP	William Whymper
EARL OF SALISBURY	John Barcroft
WELSH CAPTAIN	David Garfield
SIR PIERCE OF EXTON	Desmond Adams
GROOM	Joe Ritchie
KEEPER	Paddy Ward
ABBOT OF WESTMINSTER	Bruno Barnabé
GARDENER	Jonathan Adams
GARDENER'S MAN	Alan Collins
LORD FITZWATER	John Curless
MURDERER	Terry Wright

SERVANT	Ronald Fernee
HERALDS	Tim Brown
	Mike Lewin
QUEEN'S LADIES	Phillada Sewell
	Sandra Frieze
FIGHT ARRANGER	Terry Wright
PRODUCTION ASSISTANT	Terence Banks
PRODUCTION UNIT MANAGER	Fraser Lowden
MUSIC ADVISER	David Lloyd-Jones
LITERARY CONSULTANT	John Wilders
MAKE-UP ARTIST	Ann Rayment
COSTUME DESIGNER	Robin Fraser-Paye
SOUND	Colin Dixon
LIGHTING	John Summers
SCRIPT EDITOR	Alan Shallcross
DESIGNER	Tony Abbott
PRODUCER	Cedric Messina
DIRECTOR	David Giles

The production was recorded between 12 and 17 April 1978

THE TEXT

In order to help readers who might wish to use this text to follow the play on the screen the scene divisions and locations used in the television production and any cuts and rearrangements made are shown in the right-hand margins. The principles governing these annotations are as follows:

1. Where a new location (change of set) is used by the TV production this is shown as a new scene. The scenes are numbered consecutively and each one is identified as exterior or interior, located by a brief description of the set or the location, and placed in its 'time' setting (e.g. Day, Night, Dawn). These procedures are those used in BBC Television camera scripts.

2. Where the original stage direction shows the entry of a character at the beginning of a scene, this has not been deleted (unless it causes confusion). This is in order to demonstrate which characters are in the scene, since in most cases the TV scene begins with the characters 'discovered' on the set.

3. Where the start of a TV scene does not coincide with the start of a scene in the printed text, the characters in that scene have been listed, *unless* the start of the scene coincides with a stage direction which indicates the entrance of all those characters.

4. Where the text has been cut in the TV production, the cuts are marked by vertical rules and by a note in the margin. If complete lines are cut these are shown as, e.g., Lines 27–38 omitted. If part of a line only is cut, or in cases of doubt (e.g. in prose passages), the first and last word of the cut are also given.

5. Occasionally, and only when it is thought necessary for comprehension of the action, a note of a character's moves has been inserted in the margin.

6. Where the action moves from one part of a set to another, no attempt has been made to show this as a succession of scenes.

ALAN SHALLCROSS

29

Derek Jacobi as King Richard

RICHARD II

DRAMATIS PERSONÆ.

KING RICHARD THE SECOND.
JOHN OF GAUNT, *Duke of Lancaster,* *uncles to the King.*
EDMUND OF LANGLEY, *Duke of York.*
HENRY, *surnamed* BOLINGBROKE, *Duke of Hereford, son of John of Gaunt, afterwards King Henry IV.*
DUKE OF AUMERLE, *son of the* DUKE OF YORK.
THOMAS MOWBRAY, *Duke of Norfolk.*
DUKE OF SURREY.
EARL OF SALISBURY.
EARL BERKELEY.
BUSHY,
BAGOT, *favourites of King*
GREEN, *Richard*
EARL OF NORTHUMBERLAND.
HENRY PERCY, *surnamed* HOTSPUR, *his son*

LORD ROSS.
LORD WILLOUGHBY.
LORD FITZWATER.
BISHOP OF CARLISLE.
ABBOT OF WESTMINSTER.
LORD MARSHAL.
SIR STEPHEN SCROOP.
SIR PIERCE OF EXTON.
Captain *of a band of Welshmen.*
Two Gardeners.
QUEEN *to* KING RICHARD.
DUCHESS OF YORK.
DUCHESS OF GLOUCESTER, *widow of Thomas of Woodstock, Duke of Gloucester.*
Lady *attending on the Queen.*
Lords, Heralds, Officers, Soldiers, Keeper, Messenger, Groom, *and other* Attendants.

THE SCENE : *England and Wales.*

The Duke of Surrey and the Lord Marshal were historically the same person and are so played in the production.

ACT ONE

SCENE I. *London. The palace.*

Enter KING RICHARD, JOHN OF GAUNT, *with other* Nobles *and* Attendants.

SCENE 1
Interior. Windsor Castle. Day.

K. RICH. Old John of Gaunt, time-honoured Lancaster,
Hast thou, according to they oath and band,
Brought hither Henry Hereford, thy bold son,
Here to make good the boist'rous late appeal,
Which then our leisure would not let us hear,   5
Against the Duke of Norfolk, Thomas Mowbray ?
GAUNT. I have, my liege.
K. RICH. Tell me, moreover, hast thou sounded him
If he appeal the Duke on ancient malice,
Or worthily, as a good subject should,   10
On some known ground of treachery in him ?
GAUNT. As near as I could sift him on that argument,
On some apparent danger seen in him
Aim'd at your Highness—no inveterate malice.
K. RICH. Then call them to our presence : face to face   15
And frowning brow to brow, ourselves will hear

The accuser and the accused freely speak.
High-stomach'd are they both and full of ire,
In rage, deaf as the sea, hasty as fire.

Enter BOLINGBROKE *and* MOWBRAY.

BOLING. Many years of happy days befall   20
   My gracious sovereign, my most loving liege !
MOW. Each day still better other's happiness
   Until the heavens, envying earth's good hap,
   Add an immortal title to your crown !
K. RICH. We thank you both ; yet one but flatters us,   25
   As well appeareth by the cause you come ;
   Namely, to appeal each other of high treason.
   Cousin of Hereford, what dost thou object
   Against the Duke of Norfolk, Thomas Mowbray ?
BOLING. First—heaven be the record to my speech !   30
   In the devotion of a subject's love,
   Tend'ring the precious safety of my prince,
   And free from other misbegotten hate,
   Come I appellant to this princely presence.
   Now, Thomas Mowbray, do I turn to thee,   35
   And mark my greeting well ; for what I speak
   My body shall make good upon this earth,
   Or my divine soul answer it in heaven—
   Thou art a traitor and a miscreant,
   Too good to be so, and too bad to live,   40
   Since the more fair and crystal is the sky,
   The uglier seem the clouds that in it fly.
   Once more, the more to aggravate the note,
   With a foul traitor's name stuff I thy throat ;
   And wish—so please my sovereign—ere I move,   45
   What my tongue speaks, my right drawn sword may prove.
MOW. Let not my cold words here accuse my zeal.
   'Tis not the trial of a woman's war,
   The bitter clamour of two eager tongues,
   Can arbitrate this cause betwixt us twain ;   50
   The blood is hot that must be cool'd for this.
   Yet can I not of such tame patience boast
   As to be hush'd and nought at all to say.
   First, the fair reverence of your Highness curbs me
   From giving reins and spurs to my free speech ,   55
   Which else would post until it had return'd
   These terms of treason doubled down his throat.
   Setting aside his high blood's royalty,
   And let him be no kinsman to my liege,
   I do defy him, and I spit at him,   60
   Call him a slanderous coward and a villain ;
   Which to maintain, I would allow him odds
   And meet him, were I tied to run afoot
   Even to the frozen ridges of the Alps,
   Or any other ground inhabitable   65
   Where ever Englishman durst set his foot.
   Meantime let this defend my loyalty—
   By all my hopes, most falsely doth he lie.

BOLING. Pale trembling coward, there I throw my gage,
Disclaiming here the kindred of the King ;   70
And lay aside my high blood's royalty,
Which fear, not reverence, makes thee to except,
If guilty dread have left thee so much strength
As to take up mine honour's pawn, then stoop.
By that and all the rites of knighthood else   75
Will I make good against thee, arm to arm,
What I have spoke or thou canst worse devise.
MOW. I take it up ; and by that sword I swear
Which gently laid my knighthood on my shoulder
I'll answer thee in any fair degree   80
Or chivalrous design of knightly trial ;
And when I mount, alive may I not light
If I be traitor or unjustly fight !
K. RICH. What doth our cousin lay to Mowbray's charge ?
It must be great that can inherit us   85
So much as of a thought of ill in him.
BOLING. Look what I speak, my life shall prove it true—
That Mowbray hath receiv'd eight thousand nobles
In name of lendings for your Highness' soldiers,
The which he hath detain'd for lewd employments   90
Like a false traitor and injurious villain.
Besides, I say and will in battle prove—
Or here, or elsewhere to the furthest verge
That ever was survey'd by English eye—
That all the treasons for these eighteen years   95
Complotted and contrived in this land
Fetch from false Mowbray their first head and spring.
Further I say, and further will maintain
Upon his bad life to make all this good,
That he did plot the Duke of Gloucester's death,   100
Suggest his soon-believing adversaries,
And consequently, like a traitor coward,
Sluic'd out his innocent soul through streams of blood ;
Which blood, like sacrificing Abel's, cries,
Even from the tongueless caverns of the earth,   105
To me for justice and rough chastisement ;
And, by the glorious worth of my descent,
This arm shall do it, or this life be spent.
K. RICH. How high a pitch his resolution soars !
Thomas of Norfolk, what say'st thou to this ?   110
MOW. O, let my sovereign turn away his face
And bid his ears a little while be deaf,
Till I have told this slander of his blood
How God and good men hate so foul a liar.
K. RICH. Mowbray, impartial are our eyes and ears.   115
Were he my brother, nay, my kingdom's heir,
As he is but my father's brother's son,
Now by my sceptre's awe I make a vow,
Such neighbour nearness to our sacred blood
Should nothing privilege him nor partialize   120
The unstooping firmness of my upright soul.
He is our subject, Mowbray ; so art thou :

Free speech and fearless I to thee allow.
MOW. Then, Bolingbroke, as low as to thy heart,
    Through the false passage of thy throat, thou liest.   125
    Three parts of that receipt I had for Calais
    Disburs'd I duly to his Highness' soldiers;
    The other part reserv'd I by consent,
    For that my sovereign liege was in my debt
    Upon remainder of a dear account   130
    Since last I went to France to fetch his queen:
    Now swallow down that lie.   For Gloucester's death—
    I slew him not, but to my own disgrace
    Neglected my sworn duty in that case.
    For you, my noble Lord of Lancaster,   135
    The honourable father to my foe,
    Once did I lay an ambush for your life,
    A trespass that doth vex my grieved soul;
    But ere I last receiv'd the sacrament
    I did confess it, and exactly begg'd   140
    Your Grace's pardon; and I hope I had it.
    This is my fault.   As for the rest appeal'd,
    It issues from the rancour of a villain,
    A recreant and most degenerate traitor;
    Which in myself I boldly will defend,   145
    And interchangeably hurl down my gage
    Upon this overweening traitor's foot
    To prove myself a loyal gentleman
    Even in the best blood chamber'd in his bosom.
    In haste whereof, most heartily I pray   150
    Your Highness to assign our trial day.
K. RICH. Wrath-kindled gentlemen, be rul'd by me;
    Let's purge this choler without letting blood—
    This we prescribe, though no physician;
    Deep malice makes too deep incision.   155
    Forget, forgive; conclude and be agreed:
    Our doctors say this is no month to bleed.
    Good uncle, let this end where it begun;
    We'll calm the Duke of Norfolk, you your son.
GAUNT. To be a make-peace shall become my age.   160
    Throw down, my son, the Duke of Norfolk's gage.
K. RICH. And, Norfolk, throw down his.
GAUNT.   When, Harry, when?
    Obedience bids I should not bid again.
K. RICH. Norfolk, throw down; we bid.
    There is no boot.
MOW. Myself I throw, dread sovereign, at thy foot;   165
    My life thou shalt command, but not my shame:
    The one my duty owes; but my fair name,
    Despite of death, that lives upon my grave
    To dark dishonour's use thou shalt not have.
    I am disgrac'd, impeach'd, and baffl'd here;   170
    Pierc'd to the soul with slander's venom'd spear,
    The which no balm can cure but his heart-blood
    Which breath'd this poison.
K. RICH.   Rage must be withstood:

Give me his gage—lions make leopards tame.
MOW. Yea, but not change his spots.   Take but my shame,   175
   And I resign my gage.   My dear dear lord,
   The purest treasure mortal times afford
   Is spotless reputation ; that away,
   Men are but gilded loam or painted clay.
   A jewel in a ten-times barr'd-up chest   180
   Is a bold spirit in a loyal breast.
   Mine honour is my life ; both grow in one ;
   Take honour from me, and my life is done :
   Then, dear my liege, mine honour let me try ;
   In that I live, and for that will I die.   185
K. RICH. Cousin, throw up your gage ; do you begin.
BOLING. O, God defend my soul from such deep sin !
   Shall I seem crest-fallen in my father's sight ?
   Or with pale beggar-fear impeach my height
   Before this outdar'd dastard ? Ere my tongue   190
   Shall wound my honour with such feeble wrong
   Or sound so base a parle, my teeth shall tear
   The slavish motive of recanting fear,
   And spit it bleeding in his high disgrace,
   Where shame doth harbour, even in Mowbray's face.   195
                                         [*Exit* GAUNT.
K. RICH. We were not born to sue, but to command ;
   Which since we cannot do to make you friends,
   Be ready, as your lives shall answer it,
   At Coventry, upon Saint Lambert's day.
   There shall your swords and lances arbitrate   200
   The swelling difference of your settled hate ;
   Since we can not atone you, we shall see
   Justice design the victor's chivalry.
   Lord Marshal, command our officers-at-arms
   Be ready to direct these home alarms.   [*Exeunt.*

      SCENE II.   *London.   The Duke of Lancaster's palace.*

     Enter JOHN OF GAUNT *with the* DUCHESS OF GLOUCESTER.

GAUNT. Alas, the part I had in Woodstock's blood
   Doth more solicit me than your exclaims
   To stir against the butchers of his life !
   But since correction lieth in those hands
   Which made the fault that we cannot correct,   5
   Put we our quarrel to the will of heaven ;
   Who, when they see the hours ripe on earth,
   Will rain hot vengeance on offenders' heads.
DUCH. Finds brotherhood in thee no sharper spur ?
   Hath love in thy old blood no living fire ?   10
   Edward's seven sons, whereof thyself art one,
   Were as seven vials of his sacred blood,
   Or seven fair branches springing from one root.
   Some of those seven are dried by nature's course,
   Some of those branches by the Destinies cut ;   15
   But Thomas, my dear lord, my life, my Gloucester,
   One vial full of Edward's sacred blood,

SCENE 2
*Interior. John of
Gaunt's House. Day.*

35

One flourishing branch of his most royal root,
Is crack'd, and all the precious liquor spilt ;
Is hack'd down, and his summer leaves all faded,   20
By envy's hand and murder's bloody axe.
Ah, Gaunt, his blood was thine ! That bed, that womb,
That mettle, that self mould, that fashion'd thee,
Made him a man ; and though thou livest and breathest,
Yet art thou slain in him.   Thou dost consent   25
In some large measure to thy father's death
In that thou seest thy wretched brother die,
Who was the model of thy father's life.
Call it not patience, Gaunt—it is despair ;
In suff'ring thus thy brother to be slaught'red,   30
Thou showest the naked pathway to thy life,
Teaching stern murder how to butcher thee.
That which in mean men we entitle patience
Is pale cold cowardice in noble breasts.
What shall I say ?   To safeguard thine own life   35
The best way is to venge my Gloucester's death.
GAUNT. God's is the quarrel ; for God's substitute,
His deputy anointed in His sight,
Hath caus'd his death ; the which if wrongfully,
Let heaven revenge ; for I may never lift   40
An angry arm against His minister.
DUCH. Where then, alas, may I complain myself ?
GAUNT. To God, the widow's champion and defence.
DUCH. Why then, I will.   Farewell, old Gaunt.
Thou goest to Coventry, there to behold   45
Our cousin Hereford and fell Mowbray fight.
O, sit my husband's wrongs on Hereford's spear,
That it may enter butcher Mowbray's breast !
Or, if misfortune miss the first career,
Be Mowbray's sins so heavy in his bosom   50
That they may break his foaming courser's back
And throw the rider headlong in the lists,
A caitiff recreant to my cousin Hereford !
Farewell, old Gaunt ; thy sometimes brother's wife,
With her companion, Grief, must end her life.   55
GAUNT. Sister, farewell ; I must to Coventry.
As much good stay with thee as go with me !
DUCH. Yet one word more—grief boundeth where it falls,
Not with the empty hollowness, but weight.
I take my leave before I have begun,   60
For sorrow ends not when it seemeth done.
Commend me to thy brother, Edmund York.
Lo, this is all—nay, yet depart not so ;
Though this be all, do not so quickly go ;
I shall remember more.   Bid him—ah, what ?—   65
With all good speed at Plashy visit me.
Alack, and what shall good old York there see
But empty lodgings and unfurnish'd walls,
Unpeopled offices, untrodden stones ?
And what hear there for welcome but my groans ?   70
Therefore commend me ; let him not come there

To seek out sorrow that dwells every where.
Desolate, desolate, will I hence and die ;
The last leave of thee takes my weeping eye.   [*Exeunt.*

SCENE III.   *The lists at Coventry.*

Enter the LORD MARSHAL *and the* DUKE OF AUMERLE.

MAR.   My Lord Aumerle, is Harry Hereford arm'd ?
AUM.   Yea, at all points ; and longs to enter in.
MAR.   The Duke of Norfolk, sprightfully and bold,
   Stays but the summons of the appellant's trumpet.
AUM.   Why then, the champions are prepar'd, and stay   5
   For nothing but his Majesty's approach.

The trumpets sound, and the KING *enters with his nobles,* GAUNT, BUSHY,
   BAGOT, GREEN, *and* Others.   *When they are set, enter* MOWBRAY,
   DUKE OF NORFOLK, *in arms, defendant, and a* Herald.

K. RICH.   Marshal, demand of yonder champion
   The cause of his arrival here in arms ;
   Ask him his name ; and orderly proceed
   To swear him in the justice of his cause.   10
MAR.   In God's name and the King's, say who thou art,
   And why thou comest thus knightly clad in arms ;
   Against what man thou com'st, and what thy quarrel.
   Speak truly on thy knighthood and thy oath ;
   As so defend thee heaven and thy valour !   15
MOW.   My name is Thomas Mowbray, Duke of Norfolk ;
   Who hither come engaged by my oath—
   Which God defend a knight should violate !—
   Both to defend my loyalty and truth
   To God, my King, and my succeeding issue,   20
   Against the Duke of Hereford that appeals me ;
   And, by the grace of God and this mine arm,
   To prove him, in defending of myself,
   A traitor to my God, my King, and me.
   And as I truly fight, defend me heaven !   25

The trumpets sound.   Enter BOLINGBROKE, DUKE OF HEREFORD, *appellant,
   in armour, and a* Herald.

K. RICH.   Marshal, ask yonder knight in arms,
   Both who he is and why he cometh hither
   Thus plated in habiliments of war ;
   And formally, according to our law,
   Depose him in the justice of his cause.   30
MAR.   What is thy name ? and wherefore com'st thou hither
   Before King Richard in his royal lists ?
   Against whom comest thou ? and what's thy quarrel ?
   Speak like a true knight, so defend thee heaven !
BOLING.   Harry of Hereford, Lancaster, and Derby,   35
   Am I ; who ready here do stand in arms
   To prove, by God's grace and my body's valour,
   In lists on Thomas Mowbray, Duke of Norfolk,
   That he is a traitor, foul and dangerous,
   To God of heaven, King Richard, and to me.   40

And as I truly fight, defend me heaven !
MAR. On pain of death, no person be so bold
    Or daring-hardy as to touch the lists,
    Except the Marshal and such officers
    Appointed to direct these fair designs.   45
BOLING. Lord Marshal, let me kiss my sovereign's hand,
    And bow my knee before his Majesty ;
    For Mowbray and myself are like two men
    That vow a long and weary pilgrimage.
    Then let us take a ceremonious leave   50
    And loving farewell of our several friends.
MAR. The appellant in all duty greets your Highness,
    And craves to kiss your hand and take his leave.
K. RICH. We will descend and fold him in our arms.
    Cousin of Hereford, as thy cause is right,   55
    So be thy fortune in this royal fight !
    Farewell, my blood ; which if to-day thou shed,
    Lament we may, but not revenge thee dead.
BOLING. O, let no noble eye profane a tear
    For me, if I be gor'd with Mowbray's spear.   60
    As confident as is the falcon's flight
    Against a bird, do I with Mowbray fight.
    My loving lord, I take my leave of you ;
    Of you, my noble cousin, Lord Aumerle ;
    Not sick, although I have to do with death,   65
    But lusty, young, and cheerly drawing breath.
    Lo, as at English feasts, so I regreet
    The daintiest last, to make the end most sweet.
    O thou, the earthly author of my blood,
    Whose youthful spirit, in me regenerate,   70
    Doth with a twofold vigour lift me up
    To reach at victory above my head,
    Add proof unto mine armour with thy prayers,
    And with thy blessings steel my lance's point,
    That it may enter Mowbray's waxen coat   75
    And furbish new the name of John o' Gaunt,
    Even in the lusty haviour of his son.
GAUNT. God in thy good cause make thee prosperous !
    Be swift like lightning in the execution,
    And let thy blows, doubly redoubled,   80
    Fall like amazing thunder on the casque
    Of thy adverse pernicious enemy.
    Rouse up thy youthful blood, be valiant, and live.
BOLING. Mine innocence and Saint George to thrive !
MOW. However God or fortune cast my lot,   85
    There lives or dies, true to King Richard's throne,
    A loyal, just, and upright gentleman.
    Never did captive with a freer heart
    Cast off his chains of bondage, and embrace
    His golden uncontroll'd enfranchisement,   90
    More than my dancing soul doth celebrate
    This feast of battle with mine adversary.
    Most mighty liege, and my companion peers,
    Take from my mouth the wish of happy years.

As gentle and as jocund as to jest   95
Go I to fight : truth hath a quiet breast.
K. RICH. Farewell, my lord, securely I espy
Virtue with valour couched in thine eye.
Order the trial, Marshal, and begin.
MAR. Harry of Hereford, Lancaster, and Derby,   100
Receive thy lance ; and God defend the right !
BOLING. Strong as a tower in hope, I cry amen.
MAR. [*To an officer*.]   Go bear this lance to Thomas, Duke of Norfolk.
1 HER. Harry of Hereford, Lancaster, and Derby,
Stands here for God, his sovereign, and himself,   105
On pain to be found false and recreant,
To prove the Duke of Norfolk, Thomas Mowbray,
A traitor to his God, his King, and him ;
And dares him to set forward to the fight.
2 HER. Here standeth Thomas Mowbray, Duke of Norfolk,   110
On pain to be found false and recreant,
Both to defend himself, and to approve
Henry of Hereford, Lancaster, and Derby,
To God, his sovereign, and to him disloyal,
Courageously and with a free desire   115
Attending but the signal to begin.
MAR. Sound trumpets ; and set forward, combatants.
                                          [*A charge sounded.*
Stay, the King hath thrown his warder down.
K. RICH. Let them lay by their helmets and their spears,
And both return back to their chairs again.   120
Withdraw with us ; and let the trumpets sound
While we return these dukes what we decree.

A long flourish, while the King consults his Council.

Draw near,
And list what with our council we have done.
For that our kingdom's earth should not be soil'd   125
With that dear blood which it hath fostered ;
And for our eyes do hate the dire aspect
Of civil wounds plough'd up with neighbours' sword ;
And for we think the eagle-winged pride
Of sky-aspiring and ambitious thoughts,   130
With rival-hating envy, set on you
To wake our peace, which in our country's cradle
Draws the sweet infant breath of gentle sleep ;
Which so rous'd up with boist'rous untun'd drums,
With harsh-resounding trumpets' dreadful bray,   135
And grating shock of wrathful iron arms,
Might from our quiet confines fright fair peace
And make us wade even in our kindred's blood—
Therefore we banish you our territories.
You, cousin Hereford, upon pain of life,   140
Till twice five summers have enrich'd our fields
Shall not regreet our fair dominions,
But tread the stranger paths of banishment.
BOLING. Your will be done. This must my comfort be—
That sun that warms you here shall shine on me,   145

And those his golden beams to you here lent
Shall point on me and gild my banishment.
K. RICH. Norfolk, for thee remains a heavier doom,
Which I with some unwillingness pronounce :
The sly slow hours shall not determinate   150
The dateless limit of thy dear exile ;
The hopeless word of ' never to return '
Breathe I against thee, upon pain of life.
MOW. A heavy sentence, my most sovereign liege,
And all unlook'd for from your Highness' mouth.   155
A dearer merit, not so deep a maim
As to be cast forth in the common air,
Have I deserved at your Highness' hands.
The language I have learnt these forty years,
My native English, now I must forgo ,   160
And now my tongue's use is to me no more
Than an unstringed viol or a harp ;
Or like a cunning instrument cas'd up
Or, being open, put into his hands
That knows no touch to tune the harmony.   165
Within my mouth you have engaol'd my tongue,
Doubly portcullis'd with my teeth and lips ;
And dull, unfeeling, barren ignorance
Is made my gaoler to attend on me.
I am too old to fawn upon a nurse,   170
Too far in years to be a pupil now.
What is thy sentence, then, but speechless death,
Which robs my tongue from breathing native breath ?
K. RICH. It boots thee not to be compassionate ;
After our sentence plaining comes too late.   175
MOW. Then thus I turn me from my country's light,
To dwell in solemn shades of endless night.
K. RICH. Return again, and take an oath with thee.
Lay on our royal sword your banish'd hands ;
Swear by the duty that you owe to God,   180
Our part therein we banish with yourselves,
To keep the oath that we administer :
You never shall, so help you truth and God,
Embrace each other's love in banishment ;
Nor never look upon each other's face ;   185
Nor never write, regreet, nor reconcile
This louring tempest of your home-bred hate ;
Nor never by advised purpose meet
To plot, contrive, or complot any ill,
'Gainst us, our state, our subjects, or our land.   190
BOLING. I swear.
MOW. And I, to keep all this.
BOLING. Norfolk, so far as to mine enemy :
By this time, had the King permitted us,
One of our souls had wand'red in the air,   195
Banish'd this frail sepulchre of our flesh,
As now our flesh is banish'd from this land—
Confess thy treasons ere thou fly the realm ;
Since thou hast far to go, bear not along

The clogging burden of a guilty soul.   200
MOW. No, Bolingbroke; if ever I were traitor,
   My name be blotted from the book of life,
   And I from heaven banish'd as from hence!
   But what thou art, God, thou, and I, do know;
   And all too soon, I fear, the King shall rue.   205
   Farewell, my liege. Now no way can I stray:
   Save back to England, all the world's my way.   [*Exit.*
K. RICH. Uncle, even in the glasses of thine eyes
   I see thy grieved heart. Thy sad aspect
   Hath from the number of his banish'd years   210
   Pluck'd four away. [*To* BOLINGBROKE] Six frozen winters spent,
   Return with welcome home from banishment.
BOLING. How long a time lies in one little word!
   Four lagging winters and four wanton springs
   End in a word: such is the breath of Kings.   215
GAUNT. I thank my liege that in regard of me
   He shortens four years of my son's exile;
   But little vantage shall I reap thereby,
   For ere the six years that he hath to spend
   Can change their moons and bring their times about,   220
   My oil-dried lamp and time-bewasted light
   Shall be extinct with age and endless night;
   My inch of taper will be burnt and done,
   And blindfold death not let me see my son.
K. RICH. Why, uncle, thou hast many years to live.   225
GAUNT. But not a minute, King, that thou canst give:
   Shorten my days thou canst with sullen sorrow
   And pluck nights from me, but not lend a morrow;
   Thou can'st help time to furrow me with age,
   But stop no wrinkle in his pilgrimage;   230
   Thy word is current with him for my death,
   But dead, thy kingdom cannot buy my breath.
K. RICH. Thy son is banish'd upon good advice,
   Whereto thy tongue a party-verdict gave.
   Why at our justice seem'st thou then to lour?   235
GAUNT. Things sweet to taste prove in digestion sour.
   You urg'd me as a judge; but I had rather
   You would have bid me argue like a father.
   O, had it been a stranger, not my child,
   To smooth his fault I should have been more mild.   240
   A partial slander sought I to avoid,
   And in the sentence my own life destroy'd.
   Alas, I look'd when some of you should say
   I was too strict to make mine own away;
   But you gave leave to my unwilling tongue   245
   Against my will to do myself this wrong.
K. RICH. Cousin, farewell; and, uncle, bid him so.
   Six years we banish him, and he shall go.
                        [*Flourish.   Exit* KING *with train.*
AUM. Cousin, farewell; what presence must not know,
   From where you do remain let paper show.   250
MAR. My lord, no leave take I, for I will ride
   As far as land will let me by your side.

SCENE 4
*Interior. Bolingbroke's
Tent. Day.*
   GAUNT,
   BOLINGBROKE,
   AUMERLE, MARSHAL

41

GAUNT. O, to what purpose dost thou hoard thy words,
    That thou returnest no greeting to thy friends ?
BOLING. I have too few to take my leave of you,   255
    When the tongue's office should be prodigal
    To breathe the abundant dolour of the heart.
GAUNT. Thy grief is but thy absence for a time.
BOLING. Joy absent, grief is present for that time.
GAUNT. What is six winters ?   They are quickly gone.   260
BOLING. To men in joy ; but grief makes one hour ten.
GAUNT. Call it a travel that thou tak'st for pleasure.
BOLING. My heart will sigh when I miscall it so,
    Which finds it an enforced pilgrimage.
GAUNT. The sullen passage of thy weary steps   265
    Esteem as foil wherein thou art to set
    The precious jewel of thy home return.
BOLING. Nay, rather, every tedious stride I make
    Will but remember me what a deal of world
    I wander from the jewels that I love.   270
    Must I not serve a long apprenticehood
    To foreign passages ; and in the end,
    Having my freedom, boast of nothing else
    But that I was a journeyman to grief ?
GAUNT. All places that the eye of heaven visits   275
    Are to a wise man ports and happy havens.
    Teach thy necessity to reason thus :
    There is no virtue like necessity.
    Think not the King did banish thee,
    But thou the King.   Woe doth the heavier sit   280
    Where it perceives it is but faintly borne.
    Go, say I sent thee forth to purchase honour,
    And not the King exil'd thee ; or suppose
    Devouring pestilence hangs in our air
    And thou art flying to a fresher clime.   285
    Look what thy soul holds dear, imagine it
    To lie that way thou goest, not whence thou com'st.
    Suppose the singing birds musicians,
    The grass whereon thou tread'st the presence strew'd,
    The flowers fair ladies, and thy steps no more   290
    Than a delightful measure or a dance ;
    For gnarling sorrow hath less power to bite
    The man that mocks at it and sets it light.
BOLING. O, who can hold a fire in his hand
    By thinking on the frosty Caucasus ?   295
    Or cloy the hungry edge of appetite
    By bare imagination of a feast ?
    Or wallow naked in December snow
    By thinking on fantastic summer's heat ?
    O, no ! the apprehension of the good   300
    Gives but the greater feeling to the worse.
    Fell sorrow's tooth doth never rankle more
    Than when he bites, but lanceth not the sore.
GAUNT. Come, come, my son, I'll bring thee on thy way.
    Had I thy youth and cause, I would not stay.   305
BOLING. Then, England's ground, farewell ; sweet soil, adieu ;

My mother, and my nurse, that bears me yet !
Where'er I wander, boast of this I can :
Though banish'd, yet a trueborn English man.   [*Exeunt.*

SCENE IV. *London.   The court.*

Enter the KING, *with* BAGOT *and* GREEN, *at one door ; and the* DUKE OF
AUMERLE *at another.*

K. RICH. We did observe.   Cousin Aumerle,
  How far brought you high Hereford on his way ?
AUM. I brought high Hereford, if you call him so,
  But to the next high way, and there I left him.
K. RICH. And say, what store of parting tears were shed ?   5
AUM. Faith, none for me ; except the north-east wind,
  Which then blew bitterly against our faces,
  Awak'd the sleeping rheum, and so by chance
  Did grace our hollow parting with a tear.
K. RICH. What said our cousin when you parted with him ?   10
AUM. ' Farewell.'
  And, for my heart disdained that my tongue
  Should so profane the word, that taught me craft
  To counterfeit oppression of such grief
  That words seem'd buried in my sorrow's grave.   15
  Marry, would the word ' farewell ' have length'ned hours
  And added years to his short banishment,
  He should have had a volume of farewells ;
  But since it would not, he had none of me.
K. RICH. He is our cousin, cousin ; but 'tis doubt,   20
  When time shall call him home from banishment,
  Whether our kinsman come to see his friends.
  Ourself, and Bushy, Bagot here, and Green,
  Observ'd his courtship to the common people ;
  How he did seem to dive into their hearts   25
  With humble and familiar courtesy ;
  What reverence he did throw away on slaves,
  Wooing poor craftsmen with the craft of smiles
  And patient underbearing of his fortune,
  As 'twere to banish their affects with him.   30
  Off goes his bonnet to an oyster-wench ;
  A brace of draymen bid God speed him well
  And had the tribute of his supple knee,
  With ' Thanks, my countrymen, my loving friends ' ;
  As were our England in reversion his,   35
  And he our subjects' next degree in hope.
GREEN. Well, he is gone ; and with him go these thoughts !
  Now for the rebels which stand out in Ireland,
  Expedient manage must be made, my liege,
  Ere further leisure yield them further means   40
  For their advantage and your Highness' loss.
K. RICH. We will ourself in person to this war ;
  And, for our coffers, with too great a court
  And liberal largess, are grown somewhat light,
  We are enforc'd to farm our royal realm ;   45
  The revenue whereof shall furnish us

SCENE 5
*Interior. A Room in
the King's Palace.
Day.*

43

Jon Finch as Bolingbroke

John Gielgud as John of Gaunt and Charles Gray as the Duke of York

44

For our affairs in hand.   If that come short,
Our substitutes at home shall have blank charters ;
Whereto, when they shall know what men are rich,
They shall subscribe them for large sums of gold,   50
And send them after to supply our wants ;
For we will make for Ireland presently.

Enter BUSHY.

Bushy, what news ?
BUSHY. Old John of Gaunt is grievous sick, my lord,
Suddenly taken ; and hath sent poste-haste   55
To entreat your Majesty to visit him.
K. RICH. Where lies he ?
BUSHY. At Ely House.
K. RICH. Now put it, God, in the physician's mind
To help him to his grave immediately !   60
The lining of his coffers shall make coats
To deck our soldiers for these Irish wars.
Come, gentlemen, let's all go visit him.
Pray God we may make haste, and come too late !
ALL. Amen.   *[Exeunt.*

ACT TWO

SCENE I. *London. Ely House.*

Enter JOHN OF GAUNT, *sick, with the* DUKE OF YORK, *etc.*

SCENE 6
*Interior. Ely House.
Dusk.*

GAUNT. Will the King come, that I may breathe my last
In wholesome counsel to his unstaid youth ?
YORK. Vex not yourself, nor strive not with your breath ;
For all in vain comes counsel to his ear.
GAUNT. O, but they say the tongues of dying men   5
Enforce attention like deep harmony.
Where words are scarce, they are seldom spent in vain ;
For they breathe truth that breathe their words in pain.
He that no more must say is listen'd more
Than they whom youth and ease have taught to glose ;   10
More are men's ends mark'd than their lives before.
The setting sun, and music at the close,
As the last taste of sweets, is sweetest last,
Writ in remembrance more than things long past.
Though Richard my life's counsel would not hear,   15
My death's sad tale may yet undeaf his ear.
YORK. No ; it is stopp'd with other flattering sounds,
As praises, of whose taste the wise are fond,
Lascivious metres, to whose venom sound
The open ear of youth doth always listen ;   20
Report of fashions in proud Italy,
Whose manners still our tardy apish nation
Limps after in base imitation.
Where doth the world thrust forth a vanity—
So it be new, there's no respect how vile—   25
That is not quickly buzz'd into his ears ?
Then all too late comes counsel to be heard

Where will doth mutiny with wit's regard.
Direct not him whose way himself will choose.
'Tis breath thou lack'st, and that breath wilt thou lose.   30
GAUNT. Methinks I am a prophet new inspir'd,
  And thus expiring do foretell of him :
  His rash fierce blaze of riot cannot last,
  For violent fires soon burn out themselves ;
  Small showers last long, but sudden storms are short ;   35
  He tires betimes that spurs too fast betimes ;
  With eager feeding food doth choke the feeder ;
  Light vanity, insatiate cormorant,
  Consuming means, soon preys upon itself.
  This royal throne of kings, this scept'red isle,   40
  This earth of majesty, this seat of Mars,
  This other Eden, demi-paradise,
  This fortress built by Nature for herself
  Against infection and the hand of war,
  This happy breed of men, this little world,   45
  This precious stone set in the silver sea,
  Which serves it in the office of a wall,
  Or as a moat defensive to a house,
  Against the envy of less happier lands ;
  This blessed plot, this earth, this realm, this England,   50
  This nurse, this teeming womb of royal kings,
  Fear'd by their breed, and famous by their birth,
  Renowned for their deeds as far from home,
  For Christian service and true chivalry,
  As is the sepulchre in stubborn Jewry   55
  Of the world's ransom, blessed Mary's Son ;
  This land of such dear souls, this dear dear land,
  Dear for her reputation through the world,
  Is now leas'd out—I die pronouncing it—
  Like to a tenement or pelting farm.   60
  England, bound in with the triumphant sea,
  Whose rocky shore beats back the envious siege
  Of wat'ry Neptune, is now bound in with shame,
  With inky blots and rotten parchment bonds ;
  That England, that was wont to conquer others,   65
  Hath made a shameful conquest of itself.
  Ah, would the scandal vanish with my life,
  How happy then were my ensuing death !

Enter KING *and* QUEEN, AUMERLE, BUSHY, GREEN, BAGOT, ROSS, *and*
                WILLOUGHBY.

YORK. The King is come ; deal mildly with his youth,
  For young hot colts being rag'd do rage the more.   70
QUEEN. How fares our noble uncle Lancaster ?
K. RICH. What comfort, man ?   How is't with aged Gaunt ?
GAUNT. O, how that name befits my composition !
  Old Gaunt, indeed ; and gaunt in being old.
  Within me grief hath kept a tedious fast ;   75
  And who abstains from meat that is not gaunt ?
  For sleeping England long time have I watch'd ;
  Watching breeds leanness, leanness is all gaunt.

The pleasure that some fathers feed upon
Is my strict fast—I mean my children's looks ;   80
And therein fasting, hast thou made me gaunt.
Gaunt am I for the grave, gaunt as a grave,
Whose hollow womb inherits nought but bones.
K. RICH. Can sick men play so nicely with their names ?
GAUNT. No, misery makes sport to mock itself :   85
Since thou dost seek to kill my name in me,
I mock my name, great king, to flatter thee.
K. RICH. Should dying men flatter with those that live ?
GAUNT. No, no ; men living flatter those that die.
K. RICH Thou, now a-dying, sayest thou flatterest me.   90
GAUNT. O, no ! thou diest, though I the sicker be.
K. RICH. I am in health, I breathe, and see thee ill.
GAUNT. Now He that made me knows I see thee ill ;
Ill in myself to see, and in thee seeing ill.
Thy death-bed is no lesser than thy land   95
Wherein thou liest in reputation sick ;
And thou, too careless patient as thou art,
Commit'st thy anointed body to the cure
Of those physicians that first wounded thee :
A thousand flatterers sit within thy crown,   100
Whose compass is no bigger than thy head ;
And yet, incaged in so small a verge,
The waste is no whit lesser than thy land.
O, had thy grandsire with a prophet's eye
Seen how his son's son should destroy his sons,   105
From forth thy reach he would have laid thy shame,
Deposing thee before thou wert possess'd,
Which art possess'd now to depose thyself.
Why, cousin, wert thou regent of the world,
It were a shame to let this land by lease ;   110
But for thy world enjoying but this land,
Is it not more than shame to shame it so ?
Landlord of England art thou now, not King.
Thy state of law is bondslave to the law ;
And thou—
K. RICH.   A lunatic lean-witted fool,   115
Presuming on an ague's privilege,
Darest with thy frozen admonition
Make pale our cheek, chasing the royal blood
With fury from his native residence.
Now by my seat's right royal majesty,   120
Wert thou not brother to great Edward's son,
This tongue that runs so roundly in thy head
Should run thy head from thy unreverent shoulders.
GAUNT. O, spare me not, my brother Edward's son,
For that I was his father Edward's son ;   125
That blood already, like the pelican,
Hast thou tapp'd out, and drunkenly carous'd.
My brother Gloucester, plain well-meaning soul—
Whom fair befall in heaven 'mongst happy souls !—
May be a precedent and witness good   130
That thou respect'st not spilling Edward's blood.

Join with the present sickness that I have ;
And thy unkindness be like crooked age,
To crop at once a too long withered flower.
Live in thy shame, but die not shame with thee !   135
These words hereafter thy tormentors be !
Convey me to my bed, then to my grave.
Love they to live that love and honour have.
                        [*Exit, borne out by his* Attendants.
K. RICH. And let them die that age and sullens have ;
   For both hast thou, and both become the grave.   140
YORK. I do beseech your Majesty impute his words
   To wayward sickliness and age in him.
   He loves you, on my life, and holds you dear
   As Harry Duke of Hereford, were he here.
K. RICH. Right, you say true : as Hereford's love, so his ;   145
   As theirs, so mine ; and all be as it is.
                  Enter NORTHUMBERLAND.
NORTH. My liege, old Gaunt commends him to your Majesty.
K. RICH. What says he ?
NORTH.   Nay, nothing ; all is said.
   His tongue is now a stringless instrument ;
   Words, life, and all, old Lancaster hath spent.   150
YORK. Be York the next that must be bankrupt so !
   Though death be poor, it ends a mortal woe.
K. RICH. The ripest fruit first falls, and so doth he ;
   His time is spent, our pilgrimage must be.
   So much for that. Now for our Irish wars.   155
   We must supplant those rough rug-headed kerns,
   Which live like venom where no venom else
   But only they have privilege to live.
   And for these great affairs do ask some charge,
   Towards our assistance we do seize to us   160
   The plate, coin, revenues, and moveables,
   Whereof our uncle Gaunt did stand possess'd.
YORK. How long shall I be patient ? Ah, how long
   Shall tender duty make me suffer wrong ?
   Not Gloucester's death, nor Hereford's banishment,   165
   Nor Gaunt's rebukes, nor England's private wrongs,
   Nor the prevention of poor Bolingbroke
   About his marriage, nor my own disgrace,
   Have ever made me sour my patient cheek
   Or bend one wrinkle on my sovereign's face.   170
   I am the last of noble Edward's sons,
   Of whom thy father, Prince of Wales, was first.
   In war was never lion rag'd more fierce,
   In peace was never gentle lamb more mild,
   Than was that young and princely gentleman.   175
   His face thou hast, for even so look'd he,
   Accomplish'd with the number of thy hours ;
   But when he frown'd, it was against the French
   And not against his friends. His noble hand
   Did win what he did spend, and spent not that   180
   Which his triumphant father's hand had won.
   His hands were guilty of no kindred blood,

Mary Morris as the Duchess of Gloucester and John Gielgud as John of Gaunt

Left to right: Bagot (Damien Thomas), Green (Alan Dalton), Bushey (Robin Sachs), King Richard (Derek Jacobi), John of Gaunt (John Gielgud) and Mowbray (Richard Owens)

Left to right: Lady-in-Waiting (Sandra Frieze), Bishop of Carlisle (Clifford Rose), the Queen (Janet Maw), Lady-in-Waiting (Phillada Sewell), King Richard (Derek Jacobi), Bagot (Damien Thomas) and Green (Alan Dalton)

Janet Maw as the Queen

The Duke of Aumerle (Charles Keating), King Richard (Derek Jacobi) and the Bishop of Carlisle (Clifford Rose) on the walls of Flint Castle

Before Flint Castle. Left to right: Percy (Jeremy Bulloch), Ross (David Dodimead), Bolingbroke (Jon Finch), Willoughby (John Flint), the Duke of York (Charles Gray) and the Duke of Surrey (Jeffrey Holland)

Bolingbroke (Jon Finch) with the Duke and Duchess of York (Charles Gray and Wendy Hiller) and the Duke of Aumerle (Charles Keating)

Bolingbroke (Jon Finch) receives the crown from King Richard (Derek Jacobi)

King Richard (Derek Jacobi) takes leave of the Queen (Janet Maw)

King Richard (Derek Jacobi) with his murderers

But bloody with the enemies of his kin.
O Richard ! York is too far gone with grief,
Or else he never would compare between—   185
K. RICH. Why, uncle, what's the matter ?
YORK.   O my liege,
Pardon me, if you please ; if not, I, pleas'd
Not to be pardoned, am content withal.
Seek you to seize and gripe into your hands
The royalties and rights of banish'd Hereford ?   190
Is not Gaunt dead ? and doth not Hereford live ?
Was not Gaunt just ? and is not Harry true ?
Did not the one deserve to have an heir ?
Is not his heir a well-deserving son ?
Take Hereford's rights away, and take from Time   195
His charters and his customary rights ;
Let not to-morrow then ensue to-day ;
Be not thyself—for how art thou a king
But by fair sequence and succession ?
Now, afore God—God forbid I say true !—   200
If you do wrongfully seize Hereford's rights,
Call in the letters patents that he hath
By his attorneys-general to sue
His livery, and deny his off'red homage,
You pluck a thousand dangers on your head,   205
You lose a thousand well-disposed hearts,
And prick my tender patience to those thoughts
Which honour and allegiance cannot think.
K. RICH. Think what you will, we seize into our hands
His plate, his goods, his money, and his lands.   210
YORK. I'll not be by the while. My liege, farewell.
What will ensue hereof there's none can tell ;
But by bad courses may be understood
That their events can never fall out good.   [*Exit.*
K. RICH. Go, Bushy, to the Earl of Wiltshire straight ;   215
Bid him repair to us to Ely House
To see this business. To-morrow next
We will for Ireland ; and 'tis time, I trow.
And we create, in absence of ourself,
Our Uncle York Lord Governor of England ;   220
For he is just, and always lov'd us well.
Come on, our queen ; to-morrow must we part ;
Be merry, for our time of stay is short.
      [*Flourish. Exeunt* KING, QUEEN, BUSHY, AUMERLE, GREEN,
                                            and BAGOT.
NORTH. Well, lords, the Duke of Lancaster is dead.
ROSS. And living too ; for now his son is Duke.   225
WILLO. Barely in title, not in revenues.
NORTH. Richly in both, if justice had her right.
ROSS. My heart is great ; but it must break with silence,
Ere't be disburdened with a liberal tongue.
NORTH. Nay, speak thy mind ; and let him ne'er speak more 230
That speaks thy words again to do thee harm !
WILLO. Tends that thou wouldst speak to the Duke of Hereford ?
If it be so, out with it boldly, man ;

SCENE 7
Interior. Westminster.
The Cloisters. Day.
NORTHUMBERLAND,
ROSS, WILLOUGHBY

Quick is mine ear to hear of good towards him.
ROSS. No good at all that I can do for him ;   235
  Unless you call it good to pity him,
  Bereft and gelded of his patrimony.
NORTH. Now, afore God, 'tis shame such wrongs are borne
  In him, a royal prince and many moe
  Of noble blood in this declining land.   240
  The King is not himself, but basely led
  By flatterers ; and what they will inform,
  Merely in hate, 'gainst any of us all,
  That will the King severely prosecute
  'Gainst us, our lives, our children, and our heirs.   245
ROSS. The commons hath he pill'd with grievous taxes ;
  And quite lost their hearts ; the nobles hath he fin'd
  For ancient quarrels and quite lost their hearts.
WILLO. And daily new exactions are devis'd,
  As blanks, benevolences, and I wot not what ;   250
  But what, a God's name, doth become of this ?
NORTH. Wars hath not wasted it, for warr'd he hath not,
  But basely yielded upon compromise
  That which his noble ancestors achiev'd with blows.
  More hath he spent in peace than they in wars.   255
ROSS. The Earl of Wiltshire hath the realm in farm.
WILLO. The King's grown bankrupt like a broken man.
NORTH. Reproach and dissolution hangeth over him.
ROSS. He hath not money for these Irish wars,
  His burdenous taxations notwithstanding,   260
  But by the robbing of the banish'd Duke.
NORTH. His noble kinsman—most degenerate king !
  But, lords, we hear this fearful tempest sing,
  Yet seek no shelter to avoid the storm ;
  We see the wind sit sore upon our sails,   265
  And yet we strike not, but securely perish.
ROSS. We see the very wreck that we must suffer ;
  And unavoided is the danger now
  For suffering so the causes of our wreck.
NORTH. Not so ; even through the hollow eyes of death   270
  I spy life peering; but I dare not say
  How near the tidings of our comfort is.
WILLO. Nay, let us share thy thoughts as thou dost ours.
ROSS. Be confident to speak, Northumberland.
  We three are but thyself, and, speaking so,   275
  Thy words are but as thoughts ; therefore be bold.
NORTH. Then thus : I have from Le Port Blanc, a bay
  In Brittany, receiv'd intelligence
  That Harry Duke of Hereford, Rainold Lord Cobham,
  That late broke from the Duke of Exeter,
  His brother, Archbishop late of Canterbury,
  Sir Thomas Erpingham, Sir John Ramston,
  Sir John Norbery, Sir Robert Waterton, and Francis Quoint—
  All these, well furnish'd by the Duke of Britaine,   285
  With eight tall ships, three thousand men of war,
  Are making hither with all due expedience,
  And shortly mean to touch our northern shore.

Perhaps they had ere this, but that they stay
The first departing of the King for Ireland.   290
If then we shall shake off our slavish yoke,
Imp out our drooping country's broken wing,
Redeem from broking pawn the blemish'd crown,
Wipe off the dust that hides our sceptre's gilt,
And make high majesty look like itself,   295
Away with me in post to Ravenspurgh ;
But if you faint, as fearing to do so,
Stay and be secret, and myself will go.
ROSS. To horse, to horse ! Urge doubts to them that fear.
WILLO. Hold out my horse, and I will first be there.   [*Exeunt.*

SCENE II.   *Windsor Castle.*

Enter QUEEN, BUSHY, *and* BAGOT.

BUSHY. Madam, your Majesty is too much sad.   Lines 1–99 omitted.
   You promis'd, when you parted with the King,
   To lay aside life-harming heaviness
   And entertain a cheerful disposition.
QUEEN. To please the King, I did ; to please myself   5
   I cannot do it ; yet I know no cause
   Why I should welcome such a guest as grief,
   Save bidding farewell to so sweet a guest
   As my sweet Richard.   Yet again methinks
   Some unborn sorrow, ripe in fortune's womb,   10
   Is coming towards me, and my inward soul
   With nothing trembles.   At some thing it grieves
   More than with parting from my lord the King.
BUSHY. Each substance of a grief hath twenty shadows,
   Which shows like grief itself, but is not so ;   15
   For sorrow's eye, glazed with blinding tears,
   Divides one thing entire to many objects,
   Like perspectives which, rightly gaz'd upon,
   Show nothing but confusion—ey'd awry,
   Distinguish form.   So your sweet Majesty,   20
   Looking awry upon your lord's departure,
   Find shapes of grief more than himself to wail ;
   Which, look'd on as it is, is nought but shadows
   Of what it is not.   Then, thrice-gracious Queen,
   More than your lord's departure weep not—more is not seen : 25
   Or if it be, 'tis with false sorrow's eye,
   Which for things true weeps things imaginary.
QUEEN. It may be so ; but yet my inward soul
   Persuades me it is otherwise.   Howe'er it be,
   I cannot but be sad ; so heavy sad   30
   As—though, on thinking, on no thought I think—
   Makes me with heavy nothing faint and shrink.
BUSHY. 'Tis nothing but conceit, my gracious lady.
QUEEN. 'Tis nothing less : conceit is still deriv'd
   From some forefather grief ; mine is not so,   35
   For nothing hath begot my something grief,
   Or something hath the nothing that I grieve ;
   'Tis in reversion that I do possess—

51

But what it is that is not yet known what,
I cannot name ; 'tis nameless woe, I wot.   40

Enter GREEN.

GREEN. God save your Majesty ! and well met, gentlemen.
  I hope the King is not yet shipp'd for Ireland.
QUEEN. Why hopest thou so ? 'Tis better hope he is ;
  For his designs crave haste, his haste good hope.
  Then wherefore dost thou hope he is not shipp'd ?   45
GREEN. That he, our hope, might have retir'd his power
  And driven into despair an enemy's hope
  Who strongly hath set footing in this land.
  The banish'd Bolingbroke repeals himself,
  And with uplifted arms is safe arriv'd   50
  At Ravenspurgh.
QUEEN.   Now God in heaven forbid !
GREEN. Ah, madam, 'tis too true ; and that is worse,
  The Lord Northumberland, his son young Henry Percy,
  The Lords of Ross, Beaumond, and Willoughby,
  With all their powerful friends, are fled to him.   55
BUSHY. Why have you not proclaim'd Northumberland
  And all the rest revolted faction traitors ?
GREEN. We have ; whereupon the Earl of Worcester
  Hath broken his staff, resign'd his stewardship,
  And all the household servants fled with him   60
  To Bolingbroke.
QUEEN. So, Green, thou art the midwife to my woe,
  And Bolingbroke my sorrow's dismal heir.
  Now hath my soul brought forth her prodigy;
  And I, a gasping new-deliver'd mother,   65
  Have woe to woe, sorrow to sorrow join'd.
BUSHY. Despair not, madam.
QUEEN.   Who shall hinder me ?
  I will despair, and be at enmity
  With cozening hope—he is a flatterer,
  A parasite, a keeper-back of death,   70
  Who gently would dissolve the bands of life,
  Which false hope lingers in extremity.

Enter YORK.

GREEN. Here comes the Duke of York.
QUEEN. With signs of war about his aged neck.
  O, full of careful business are his looks !   75
  Uncle, for God's sake, speak comfortable words.
YORK. Should I do so, I should belie my thoughts.
  Comfort's in heaven ; and we are on the earth,
  Where nothing lives but crosses, cares, and grief.
  Your husband, he is gone to save far off,   80
  Whilst others come to make him lose at home.
  Here am I left to underprop his land,
  Who, weak with age, cannot support myself.
  Now comes the sick hour that his surfeit made ;
  Now shall he try his friends that flatter'd him.   85

Enter a Servingman.

SERV. My lord, your son was gone before I came.
YORK. He was—why so go all which way it will!
   The nobles they are fled, the commons they are cold
   And will, I fear, revolt on Hereford's side.
   Sirrah, get thee to Plashy, to my sister Gloucester ;   90
   Bid her send me presently a thousand pound.
   Hold, take my ring.
SERV. My lord, I had forgot to tell your lordship,
   To-day, as I came by, I called there—
   But I shall grieve you to report the rest.   95
YORK. What is't, knave ?
SERV. An hour before I came, the Duchess died.
YORK. God for his mercy ! what a tide of woes
   Comes rushing on this woeful land at once !
   I know not what to do. I would to God,   100
   So my untruth had not provok'd him to it,
   The King had cut off my head with my brother's.
   What, are there no posts dispatch'd for Ireland ?
   How shall we do for money for these wars ?
   Come, sister—cousin, I would say—pray, pardon me.   105
   Go, fellow, get thee home, provide some carts,
   And bring away the armour that is there.   [*Exit* Servingman.
   Gentlemen, will you go muster men ?
   If I know how or which way to order these affairs
   Thus disorderly thrust into my hands,   110
   Never believe me. Both are my kinsmen.
   T'one is my sovereign, whom both my oath
   And duty bids defend ; t'other again
   Is my kinsman, whom the King hath wrong'd,
   Whom conscience and my kindred bids to right.   115
   Well, somewhat we must do.—Come, cousin,
   I'll dispose of you. Gentlemen, go muster up your men
   And meet me presently at Berkeley.
   I should to Plashy too,   120
   But time will not permit. All is uneven,
   And everything is left at six and seven. [*Exeunt* YORK *and* QUEEN.
BUSHY. The wind sits fair for news to go to Ireland.
   But none returns. For us to levy power
   Proportionable to the enemy   125
   Is all unpossible.
GREEN. Besides, our nearness to the King in love
   Is near the hate of those love not the King.
BAGOT. And that is the wavering commons ; for their love
   Lies in their purses ; and whoso empties them,   130
   By so much fills their hearts with deadly hate.
BUSHY. Wherein the King stands generally condemn'd.
BAGOT. If judgment lie in them, then so do we,
   Because we ever have been near the King.
GREEN. Well, I will for refuge straight to Bristow Castle.   135
   The Earl of Wiltshire is already there.
BUSHY. Thither will I with you ; for little office
   Will the hateful commons perform for us,
   Except like curs to tear us all to pieces.
   Will you go along with us ?   140

Lines 1–99 omitted

SCENE 8
*Interior. Windsor
Castle. Day.*
YORK, THE QUEEN,
BUSHY, BAGOT, GREEN

Exeunt YORK *and*
QUEEN.
Lines 120–122
omitted.

BAGOT. No ; I will to Ireland to his Majesty.
  Farewell.   If heart's presages be not vain,
  We three here part that ne'er shall meet again.
BUSHY. That's as York thrives to beat back Bolingbroke.
GREEN Alas, poor Duke ! the task he undertakes   **145**
  Is numb'ring sands and drinking oceans dry.
  Where one on his side fights, thousands will fly.
  Farewell at once—for once, for all, and ever.
BUSHY. Well, we may meet again.
BAGOT.   I fear me, never.   *[Exeunt.*

SCENE III.   *Gloucestershire.*

Enter BOLINGBROKE *and* NORTHUMBERLAND, *with* Forces.

SCENE 9
Exterior.
Gloucestershire. Dusk.

BOLING. How far is it, my lord, to Berkeley now ?
NORTH. Believe me, noble lord,
  I am a stranger here in Gloucestershire.
  These high wild hills and rough uneven ways
  Draws out our miles, and makes them wearisome ;   **5**
  And yet your fair discourse hath been as sugar,
  Making the hard way sweet and delectable.
  But I bethink me what a weary way
  From Ravenspurgh to Cotswold will be found
  In Ross and Willoughby, wanting your company,   **10**
  Which, I protest, hath very much beguil'd
  The tediousness and process of my travel.
  But theirs is sweet'ned with the hope to have
  The present benefit which I possess .
  And hope to joy is little less in joy   **15**
  Than hope enjoy'd.   By this the weary lords
  Shall make their way seem short, as mine hath done
  By sight of what I have, your noble company.
BOLING. Of much less value is my company
  Than your good words.   But who comes here ?   **20**

Enter HARRY PERCY.

NORTH. It is my son, young Harry Percy,
  Sent from my brother Worcester, whencesoever.
  Harry, how fares your uncle ?
PERCY. I had thought, my lord, to have learn'd his health of you.
NORTH. Why, is he not with the Queen ?   **25**
PERCY. No, my good lord ; he hath forsook the court,
  Broken his staff of office, and dispers'd
  The household of the King.
NORTH.   What was his reason ?
  He was not so resolv'd when last we spake together.
PERCY. Because your lordship was proclaimed traitor.   **30**
  But he, my lord, is gone to Ravenspurgh,
  To offer service to the Duke of Hereford ;
  And sent me over by Berkeley, to discover
  What power the Duke of York had levied there ;
  Then with directions to repair to Ravenspurgh.   **35**
NORTH. Have you forgot the Duke of Hereford, boy ?
PERCY. No, my good lord ; for that is not forgot

54

Which ne'er I did remember ; to my knowledge,
I never in my life did look on him.
NORTH. Then learn to know him now ; this is the Duke.   40
PERCY. My gracious lord, I tender you my service,
  Such as it is, being tender, raw, and young ;
  Which elder days shall ripen, and confirm
  To more approved service and desert.
BOLING. I thank thee, gentle Percy ; and be sure   45
  I count myself in nothing else so happy
  As in a soul rememb'ring my good friends ;
  And as my fortune ripens with thy love,
  It shall be still thy true love's recompense.
  My heart this covenant makes, my hand thus seals it.   50
NORTH. How far is it to Berkeley ? And what stir
  Keeps good old York there with his men of war ?
PERCY. There stands the castle, by yon tuft of trees,
  Mann'd with three hundred men, as I have heard ;
  And in it are the Lords of York, Berkeley, and Seymour—   55
  None else of name and noble estimate.

                Enter ROSS *and* WILLOUGHBY.

NORTH. Here come the Lords of Ross and Willoughby,
  Bloody with spurring, fiery-red with haste.
BOLING. Welcome, my lords. I wot your love pursues
  A banish'd traitor. All my treasury   60
  Is yet but unfelt thanks, which, more enrich'd,
  Shall be your love and labour's recompense.
ROSS. Your presence makes us rich, most noble lord.
WILLO. And far surmounts our labour to attain it.
BOLING. Evermore thanks, the exchequer of the poor ;   65
  Which, till my infant fortune comes to years,
  Stands for my bounty. But who comes here ?

                Enter BERKELEY.

NORTH. It is my Lord of Berkeley, as I guess.
BERK. My Lord of Hereford, my message is to you.
BOLING. My lord, my answer is—' to Lancaster ' ;   70
  And I am come to seek that name in England ;
  And I must find that title in your tongue
  Before I make reply to aught you say.
BERK. Mistake me not, my lord ; 'tis not my meaning
  To raze one title of your honour out.   75
  To you, my lord, I come—what lord you will—
  From the most gracious regent of this land,
  The Duke of York, to know what pricks you on
  To take advantage of the absent time,
  And fright our native peace with self-borne arms.   80

                Enter YORK, *attended.*

BOLING. I shall not need transport my words by you ;
  Here comes his Grace in person. My noble uncle   [*Kneels.*
YORK. Show me thy humble heart, and not thy knee,
  Whose duty is deceivable and false.
BOLING. My gracious uncle !—   85

YORK. Tut, tut!
  Grace me no grace, nor uncle me no uncle.
  I am no traitor's uncle; and that word ' grace '
  In an ungracious mouth is but profane.
  Why have those banish'd and forbidden legs   90
  Dar'd once to touch a dust of England's ground?
  But then more ' why? '—why have they dar'd to march
  So many miles upon her peaceful bosom,
  Frighting her pale-fac'd villages with war
  And ostentation of despised arms?   95
  Com'st thou because the anointed King is hence?
  Why, foolish boy, the King is left behind,
  And in my loyal bosom lies his power.
  Were I but now lord of such hot youth
  As when brave Gaunt, thy father, and myself   100
  Rescued the Black Prince, that young Mars of men,
  From forth the ranks of many thousand French,
  O, then how quickly should this arm of mine,
  Now prisoner to the palsy, chastise thee
  And minister correction to thy fault!   105
BOLING. My gracious uncle, let me know my fault;
  On what condition stands it and wherein?
YORK. Even in condition of the worst degree—
  In gross rebellion and detested treason.
  Thou art a banish'd man, and here art come   110
  Before the expiration of thy time,
  In braving arms against thy sovereign.
BOLING. As I was banish'd, I was banish'd Hereford;
  But as I come, I come for Lancaster.
  And, noble uncle, I beseech your Grace   115
  Look on my wrongs with an indifferent eye.
  You are my father, for methinks in you
  I see old Gaunt alive. O, then, my father,
  Will you permit that I shall stand condemn'd
  A wandering vagabond; my rights and royalties   120
  Pluck'd from my arms perforce, and given away
  To upstart unthrifts? Wherefore was I born?
  If that my cousin king be King in England,
  It must be granted I am Duke of Lancaster.
  You have a son, Aumerle, my noble cousin;   125
  Had you first died, and he been thus trod down,
  He should have found his uncle Gaunt a father
  To rouse his wrongs and chase them to the bay.
  I am denied to sue my livery here,
  And yet my letters patents give me leave.   130
  My father's goods are all distrain'd and sold;
  And these and all are all amiss employ'd.
  What would you have me do? I am a subject,
  And I challenge law—attorneys are denied me;
  And therefore personally I lay my claim   135
  To my inheritance of free descent.
NORTH. The noble Duke hath been too much abused.
ROSS. It stands your Grace upon to do him right.
WILLO. Base men by his endowments are made great.

YORK. My lords of England, let me tell you this :   140
    I have had feeling of my cousin's wrongs,
    And labour'd all I could to do him right ;
    But in this kind to come, in braving arms,
    Be his own carver and cut out his way,
    To find out right with wrong—it may not be ;   145
    And you that do abet him in this kind
    Cherish rebellion, and are rebels all.
NORTH. The noble Duke hath sworn his coming is
    But for his own ; and for the right of that
    We all have strongly sworn to give him aid ;   150
    And let him never see joy that breaks that oath !
YORK. Well, well, I see the issue of these arms.
    I cannot mend it, I must needs confess,
    Because my power is weak and all ill left ;
    But if I could, by Him that gave me life,   155
    I would attach you all and make you stoop
    Unto the sovereign mercy of the King ;
    But since I cannot, be it known unto you
    I do remain as neuter.   So, fare you well ;
    Unless you please to enter in the castle,   160
    And there repose you for this night.
BOLING. An offer, uncle, that we will accept.
    But we must win your Grace to go with us
    To Bristow Castle, which they say is held
    By Bushy, Bagot, and their complices,   165
    The caterpillars of the commonwealth,
    Which I have sworn to weed and pluck away.
YORK. It may be I will go with you ; but yet I'll pause,
    For I am loath to break our country's laws.
    Nor friends nor foes, to me welcome you are.   170
    Things past redress are now with me past care.   [*Exeunt.*

SCENE IV.   *A camp in Wales.*

Enter EARL OF SALISBURY *and a* Welsh Captain.

SCENE 10
*Exterior. A Camp
in Wales. Night.*

CAP. My Lord of Salisbury, we have stay'd ten days
    And hardly kept our countrymen together,
    And yet we hear no tidings from the King ;
    Therefore we will disperse ourselves.   Farewell.
SAL. Stay yet another day, thou trusty Welshman ;   5
    The king reposeth all his confidence in thee.
CAP. 'Tis thought the King is dead ; we will not stay.
    The bay trees in our country are all wither'd,
    And meteors fright the fixed stars of heaven ;
    The pale-fac'd moon looks bloody on the earth,   10
    And lean-look'd prophets whisper fearful change ;
    Rich men look sad, and ruffians dance and leap—
    The one in fear to lose what they enjoy,
    The other to enjoy by rage and war.
    These signs forerun the death or fall of kings.   15
    Farewell.   Our countrymen are gone and fled,
    As well assur'd Richard their King is dead.   [*Exit.*
| SAL. Ah, Richard, with the eyes of heavy mind,

| Lines 18–24 omitted.

I see thy glory like a shooting star
Fall to the base earth from the firmament !   20
The sun sets weeping in the lowly west,
Witnessing storms to come, woe, and unrest ;
Thy friends are fled, to wait upon thy foes ;
And crossly to thy good all fortune goes.   [*Exit.*

Lines 18–24 omitted.

ACT THREE

SCENE I. *Bolingbroke's camp at Bristol.*

Enter BOLINGBROKE, YORK, NORTHUMBERLAND, PERCY, ROSS,
WILLOUGHBY, *with* BUSHY *and* GREEN, prisoners.

SCENE 11
*Exterior. Outside
Bolingbroke's Tent.
Night.*
Line 1 omitted.

BOLING. Bring forth these men.
      Bushy and Green, I will not vex your souls—
      Since presently your souls must part your bodies—
      With too much urging your pernicious lives,
      For 'twere no charity ; yet, to wash your blood   5
      From off my hands, here in the view of men
      I will unfold some causes of your deaths :
      You have misled a prince, a royal king,
      A happy gentleman in blood and lineaments,
      By you unhappied and disfigured clean ;   10
      You have in manner with your sinful hours
      Made a divorce betwixt his queen and him ;
      Broke the possession of a royal bed,
      And stain'd the beauty of a fair queen's cheeks
      With tears drawn from her eyes by your foul wrongs ;   15
      Myself—a prince by fortune of my birth,
      Near to the King in blood, and near in love
      Till you did make him misinterpret me—
      Have stoop'd my neck under your injuries
      And sigh'd my English breath in foreign clouds,   20
      Eating the bitter bread of banishment,
      Whilst you have fed upon my signories,
      Dispark'd my parks and fell'd my forest woods,
      From my own windows torn my household coat,
      Raz'd out my imprese, leaving me no sign   25
      Save men's opinions and my living blood
      To show the world I am a gentleman.
      This and much more, much more than twice all this,
      Condemns you to the death.   See them delivered over
      To execution and the hand of death.   30
BUSHY. More welcome is the stroke of death to me
      Than Bolingbroke to England.   Lords, farewell.
GREEN. My comfort is that heaven will take our souls,
      And plague injustice with the pains of hell.
BOLING. My Lord Northumberland, see them dispatch'd.   35
               [*Exeunt Northumberland, and others,* with the
                                                     prisoners.

      Uncle, you say the Queen is at your house ;
      For God's sake, fairly let her be entreated.
      Tell her I send to her my kind commends ;
      Take special care my greetings be delivered.

YORK. A gentleman of mine I have dispatch'd   40
   With letters of your love to her at large.
BOLING. Thanks, gentle uncle.   Come, lords, away,
   To fight with Glendower and his complices.
   Awhile to work, and after holiday.   [*Exeunt.*

SCENE II.   *The coast of Wales.   A castle in view.*

Drums.   Flourish and colours.   Enter the KING, *the* BISHOP OF CARLISLE
              AUMERLE *and* Soldiers.

K. RICH. Barkloughly Castle call they this at hand ?
AUM. Yea, my lord.   How brooks your Grace the air
   After your late tossing on the breaking seas ?
K. RICH. Needs must I like it well.   I weep for joy
   To stand upon my kingdom once again.   5
   Dear earth, I do salute thee with my hand,
   Though rebels wound thee with their horses' hoofs.
   As a long-parted mother with her child
   Plays fondly with her tears and smiles in meeting,
   So weeping-smiling greet I thee, my earth,   10
   And do thee favours with my royal hands.
   Feed not thy sovereign's foe, my gentle earth,
   Nor with thy sweets comfort his ravenous sense ;
   But let thy spiders, that suck up thy venom,
   And heavy-gaited toads, lie in their way,   15
   Doing annoyance to the treacherous feet
   Which with usurping steps do trample thee ;
   Yield stinging nettles to mine enemies ;
   And when they from thy bosom pluck a flower,
   Guard it, I pray thee, with a lurking adder,   20
   Whose double tongue may with a mortal touch
   Throw death upon thy sovereign's enemies.
   Mock not my senseless conjuration, lords.
   This earth shall have a feeling, and these stones
   Prove armed soldiers, ere her native King   25
   Shall falter under foul rebellion's arms.
CAR. Fear not, my lord ; that Power that made you king
   Hath power to keep you king in spite of all.
   The means that heaven yields must be embrac'd
   And not neglected ; else, if heaven would,   30
   And we will not, heaven's offer we refuse,
   The proffered means of succour and redress.
AUM. He means, my lord, that we are too remiss ;
   Whilst Bolingbroke, through our security,
   Grows strong and great in substance and in power.   35
K. RICH. Discomfortable cousin ! know'st thou not
   That when the searching eye of heaven is hid,
   Behind the globe, that lights the lower world,
   Then thieves and robbers range abroad unseen
   In murders and in outrage boldly here ;   40
   But when from under this terrestrial ball
   He fires the proud tops of the eastern pines
   And darts his light through every guilty hole,
   Then murders, treasons, and detested sins,

SCENE 12
*Exterior. The Coast
of Wales. Night.*

The cloak of night being pluck'd from off their backs,   45
Stand bare and naked, trembling at themselves?
So when this thief, this traitor, Bolingbroke,
Who all this while hath revell'd in the night,
Whilst we were wand'ring with the Antipodes,
Shall see us rising in our throne, the east,   50
His treasons will sit blushing in his face,
Not able to endure the sight of day,
But self-affrighted tremble at his sin.
Not all the water in the rough rude sea
Can wash the balm off from an anointed king;   55
The breath of worldly men cannot depose
The deputy elected by the Lord.
For every man that Bolingbroke hath press'd
To lift shrewd steel against our golden crown,
God for his Richard hath in heavenly pay   60
A glorious angel.   Then, if angels fight,
Weak men must fall; for heaven still guards the right.

Enter SALISBURY.

Welcome, my lord.   How far off lies your power?
SAL. Nor near nor farther off, my gracious lord,
Than this weak arm.   Discomfort guides my tongue,   65
And bids me speak of nothing but despair.
One day too late, I fear me, noble lord,
Hath clouded all thy happy days on earth.
O, call back yesterday, bid time return,
And thou shalt have twelve thousand fighting men!   70
To-day, to-day, unhappy day, too late,
O'erthrows thy joys, friends, fortune, and thy state;
For all the Welshmen, hearing thou wert dead,
Are gone to Bolingbroke, dispers'd, and fled.
AUM. Comfort, my liege, why looks your Grace so pale?   75
K. RICH. But now the blood of twenty thousand men
Did triumph in my face, and they are fled;
And, till so much blood thither come again,
Have I not reason to look pale and dead?
All souls that will be safe, fly from my side;   80
For time hath set a blot upon my pride.
AUM. Comfort, my liege; remember who you are.
K. RICH. I had forgot myself; am I not King?
Awake, thou coward majesty! thou sleepest.
Is not the King's name twenty thousand names?   85
Arm, arm, my name! a puny subject strikes
At thy great glory.   Look not to the ground,
Ye favourites of a king; are we not high?
High be our thoughts.   I know my uncle York
Hath power enough to serve our turn.   But who comes here? 90

Enter SCROOP.

SCROOP. More health and happiness betide my liege
Than can my care-tun'd tongue deliver him.
K. RICH. Mine ear is open and my heart prepar'd.
The worst is worldly loss thou canst unfold.
Say, is my kingdom lost?   Why, 'twas my care;   95

And what loss is it to be rid of care ?
Strives Bolingbroke to be as great as we ?
Greater he shall not be ; if he serve God,
We'll serve him too, and be his fellow so.
Revolt our subjects ?   That we cannot mend ;   100
They break their faith to God as well as us.
Cry woe, destruction, ruin, and decay—
The worst is death, and death will have his day.
SCROOP. Glad am I that your Highness is so arm'd
To bear the tidings of calamity.   105
Like an unseasonable stormy day
Which makes the silver rivers drown their shores,
As if the world were all dissolv'd to tears,
So high above his limits swells the rage
Of Bolingbroke, covering your fearful land   110
With hard bright steel and hearts harder than steel.
White-beards have arm'd their thin and hairless scalps
Against thy majesty ; boys, with women's voices,
Strive to speak big, and clap their female joints
In stiff unwieldy arms against thy crown ;   115
Thy very beadsmen learn to bend their bows
Of double-fatal yew against thy state ;
Yea, distaff-women manage rusty bills
Against thy seat : both young and old rebel,
And all goes worse than I have power to tell.   120
K. RICH. Too well, too well thou tell'st a tale so ill.
Where is the Earl of Wiltshire ?   Where is Bagot ?
What is become of Bushy ?   Where is Green ?
That they have let the dangerous enemy
Measure our confines with such peaceful steps ?   125
If we prevail, their heads shall pay for it.
I warrant they have made peace with Bolingbroke.
SCROOP. Peace have they made with him indeed, my lord.
K. RICH. O villains, vipers, damn'd without redemption !
Dogs, easily won to fawn on any man !   130
Snakes, in my heart-blood warm'd, that sting my heart !
Three Judases, each one thrice worse than Judas !
Would they make peace ?   Terrible hell make war
Upon their spotted souls for this offence !
SCROOP. Sweet love, I see, changing his property,   135
Turns to the sourrest and most deadly hate.
Again uncurse their souls ; their peace is made
With heads, and not with hands ; those whom you curse
Have felt the worst of death's destroying wound
And lie full low, grav'd in the hollow ground.   140
AUM. Is Bushy, Green, and the Earl of Wiltshire dead ?
SCROOP. Ay, all of them at Bristow lost their heads.
AUM. Where is the Duke my father with his power ?
K. RICH. No matter where—of comfort no man speak.
Let's talk of graves, of worms, and epitaphs ;   145
Make dust our paper, and with rainy eyes
Write sorrow on the bosom of the earth.
Let's choose executors and talk of wills ;
And yet not so—for what can we bequeath

Save our deposed bodies to the ground ?   150
Our lands, our lives, and all, are Bolingbroke's.
And nothing can we call our own but death
And that small model of the barren earth
Which serves as paste and cover to our bones.
For God's sake let us sit upon the ground   155
And tell sad stories of the death of kings :
How some have been depos'd, some slain in war,
Some haunted by the ghosts they have depos'd,
Some poison'd by their wives, some sleeping kill'd,
All murder'd—for within the hollow crown   160
That rounds the mortal temples of a king
Keeps Death his court ; and there the antic sits,
Scoffing his state and grinning at his pomp ;
Allowing him a breath, a little scene,
To monarchize, be fear'd, and kill with looks ;   165
Infusing him with self and vain conceit,
As if this flesh which walls about our life
Were brass impregnable ; and, humour'd thus,
Comes at the last, and with a little pin
Bores through his castle wall, and farewell, king !   170
Cover your heads, and mock not flesh and blood
With solemn reverence ; throw away respect,
Tradition, form, and ceremonious duty ;
For you have but mistook me all this while.
I live with bread like you, feel want,   175
Taste grief, need friends : subjected thus,
How can you say to me I am a king ?
CAR. My lord, wise men ne'er sit and wail their woes,
But presently prevent the ways to wail.
To fear the foe, since fear oppresseth strength,   180
Gives, in your weakness, strength unto your foe,
And so your follies fight against yourself.
Fear and be slain—no worse can come to fight ;
And fight and die is death destroying death,
Where fearing dying pays death servile breath.   185
AUM. My father hath a power ; inquire of him,
And learn to make a body of a limb.
K. RICH. Thou chid'st me well. Proud Bolingbroke, I come
To change blows with thee for our day of doom.
This ague fit of fear is over-blown ;   190
An easy task it is to win our own.
Say, Scroop, where lies our uncle with his power ?
Speak sweetly, man, although thy looks be sour.
SCROOP. Men judge by the complexion of the sky
The state and inclination of the day ;   195
So may you by my dull and heavy eye,
My tongue hath but a heavier tale to say.
I play the torturer, by small and small
To lengthen out the worst that must be spoken :
Your uncle York is join'd with Bolingbroke ;   200
And all your northern castles yielded up,
And all your southern gentlemen in arms
Upon his party.

K. RICH.   Thou hast said enough.
   [*To* AUMERLE.]   Beshrew thee, cousin, which didst lead me forth
Of that sweet way I was in to despair !
What say you now ?   What comfort have we now ?
By heaven, I'll hate him everlastingly
That bids me be of comfort any more.
Go to Flint Castle ; there I'll pine away ;
A king, woe's slave, shall kingly woe obey.   210
That power I have, discharge ; and let them go
To ear the land that hath some hope to grow,
For I have none.   Let no man speak again
To alter this, for counsel is but vain.
AUM. My liege, one word.
K. RICH.   He does me double wrong   215
   That wounds me with the flatteries of his tongue.
Discharge my followers ; let them hence away,
From Richard's night to Bolingbroke's fair day.   [*Exeunt.*

SCENE III.   Wales.   Before Flint Castle.

Enter, with drum and colours, BOLINGBROKE, YORK, NORTHUMBERLAND,
and Forces.

BOLING. So that by this intelligence we learn
   The Welshmen are dispers'd ; and Salisbury
Is gone to meet the King, who lately landed
With some few private friends upon this coast.
NORTH. The news is very fair and good, my lord.   5
   Richard not far from hence hath hid his head.
YORK. It would beseem the Lord Northumberland
   To say ' King Richard '.   Alack the heavy day
When such a sacred king should hide his head !
NORTH. Your Grace mistakes ; only to be brief,   10
   Left I his title out.
YORK.   The time hath been,
   Would you have been so brief with him, he would
Have been so brief with you to shorten you,
For taking so the head, your whole head's length.
BOLING. Mistake not, uncle, further than you should.   15
YORK. Take not, good cousin, further than you should,
   Lest you mistake.   The heavens are over our heads.
BOLING. I know it, uncle ; and oppose not myself
   Against their will.   But who comes here ?

Enter PERCY.

Welcome, Harry.   What, will not this castle yield ?   20
PERCY. The castle royally is mann'd, my lord,
   Against thy entrance.
BOLING. Royally !
   Why, it contains no king ?
PERCY.   Yes, my good lord,
   It doth contain a king ; King Richard lies
Within the limits of yon lime and stone ;   25
And with him are the Lord Aumerle, Lord Salisbury,
Sir Stephen Scroop, besides a clergyman

SCENE 13
*Interior. Bolingbroke's
Tent before Flint
Castle. Night.*

Of holy reverence ; who, I cannot learn.
NORTH. O, belike it is the Bishop of Carlisle.   30
BOLING. [*To* NORTHUMBERLAND.] Noble lord,
Go to the rude ribs of that ancient castle ;
Through brazen trumpet send the breath of parley
Into his ruin'd ears, and thus deliver :
Henry Bolingbroke   35
On both his knees doth kiss King Richard's hand,
And sends allegiance and true faith of heart
To his most royal person ; hither come
Even at his feet to lay my arms and power,
Provided that my banishment repeal'd   40
And lands restor'd again be freely granted ;
If not, I'll use the advantage of my power
And lay the summer's dust with showers of blood
Rain'd from the wounds of slaughtered Englishmen ;
The which how far off from the mind of Bolingbroke   45
It is such crimson tempest should bedrench
The fresh green lap of fair King Richard's land,
My stooping duty tenderly shall show.
Go, signify as much, while here we march
Upon the grassy carpet of this plain.   50
          [NORTHUMBERLAND *advances to the Castle,*
                                with a trumpet.
Let's march without the noise of threat'ning drum,
That from this castle's tottered battlements
Our fair appointments may be well perus'd.
Methinks King Richard and myself should meet
With no less terror than the elements   55
Of fire and water, when their thund'ring shock
At meeting tears the cloudy cheeks of heaven.
Be he the fire, I'll be the yielding water ;
The rage be his, whilst on the earth I rain
My waters—on the earth, and not on him.   60
March on, and mark King Richard how he looks.

Parle without, and answer within ; then a flourish. Enter on the walls,   SCENE 14
the KING, *the* BISHOP OR CARLISLE, AUMERLE, SCROOP *and* SALISBURY.   *Exterior. Before Flint*
                                                                  Castle. Night.
See, see, King Richard doth himself appear,
As doth the blushing discontented sun
From out the fiery portal of the east,
When he perceives the envious clouds are bent   65
To dim his glory and to stain the track
Of his bright passage to the occident.
YORK. Yet looks he like a king. Behold, his eye,
As bright as is the eagle's, lightens forth
Controlling majesty. Alack, alack, for woe,   70
That any harm should stain so fair a show !
K. RICH. [*To* NORTHUMBERLAND.] We are amaz'd ; and thus long have
    we stood
To watch the fearful bending of thy knee,
Because we thought ourself the lawful king ;
And if we be, how dare thy joints forget   75
To pay their awful duty to our presence ?

If we be not, show us the hand of God
That hath dismiss'd us from our stewardship;
For well we know no hand of blood and bone
Can gripe the sacred handle of our sceptre,   80
Unless he do profane, steal, or usurp.
And though you think that all, as you have done,
Have torn their souls by turning them from us,
And we are barren and bereft of friends,
Yet know—my master, God omnipotent,   85
Is mustering in his clouds on our behalf
Armies of pestilence; and they shall strike
Your children yet unborn and unbegot,
That lift your vassal hands against my head
And threat the glory of my precious crown.   90
Tell Bolingbroke, for yon methinks he stands,
That every stride he makes upon my land
Is dangerous treason; he is come to open
The purple testament of bleeding war;
But ere the crown he looks for live in peace,   95
Ten thousand bloody crowns of mothers' sons
Shall ill become the flower of England's face,
Change the complexion of her maid-pale peace
To scarlet indignation, and bedew
Her pastures' grass with faithful English blood.   100
NORTH. The King of Heaven forbid our lord the King
Should so with civil and uncivil arms
Be rush'd upon!   Thy thrice noble cousin,
Harry Bolingbroke, doth humbly kiss thy hand;
And by the honourable tomb he swears   105
That stands upon your royal grandsire's bones,
And by the royalties of both your bloods,
Currents that spring from one most gracious head,
And by the buried hand of warlike Gaunt,
And by the worth and honour of himself,   110
Comprising all that may be sworn or said,
His coming hither hath no further scope
Than for his lineal royalties, and to beg
Enfranchisement immediate on his knees;
Which on thy royal party granted once,   115
His glittering arms he will commend to rust,
His barbed steeds to stables, and his heart
To faithful service of your Majesty.
This swears he, as he is a prince, is just;
And as I am a gentleman I credit him.   120
K. RICH. Northumberland, say thus the King returns:
His noble cousin is right welcome hither;
And all the number of his fair demands
Shall be accomplish'd without contradiction.
With all the gracious utterance thou hast   125
Speak to his gentle hearing kind commends.
[To AUMERLE.] We do debase ourselves, cousin, do we not,
To look so poorly and to speak so fair?
Shall we call back Northumberland, and send
Defiance to the traitor, and so die?   130

AUM. No, good my lord ; let's fight with gentle words
    Till time lend friends, and friends their helpful swords.
K. RICH. O God, O God ! that e'er this tongue of mine
    That laid the sentence of dread banishment
    On yon proud man should take it off again   135
    With words of sooth !   O that I were as great
    As is my grief, or lesser than my name !
    Or that I could forget what I have been !
    Or not remember what I must be now !
    Swell'st thou, proud heart ?   I'll give thee scope to beat, 140
    Since foes have scope to beat both thee and me.
AUM. Northumberland comes back from Bolingbroke.
K. RICH. What must the King do now ?   Must he submit ?
    The King shall do it.   Must he be depos'd ?
    The King shall be contented.   Must he lose   145
    The name of king ?   A God's name, let it go.
    I'll give my jewels for a set of beads,
    My gorgeous palace for a hermitage,
    My gay apparel for an almsman's gown,
    My figur'd goblets for a dish of wood,   150
    My sceptre for a palmer's walking staff,
    My subjects for a pair of carved saints,
    And my large kingdom for a little grave,
    A little little grave, an obscure grave—
    Or I'll be buried in the king's high way,   155
    Some way of common trade, where subjects' feet
    May hourly trample on their sovereign's head ;
    For on my heart they tread now whilst I live,
    And buried once, why not upon my head ?
    Aumerle, thou weep'st, my tender-hearted cousin !   160
    We'll make foul weather with despised tears ;
    Our sighs and they shall lodge the summer corn
    And make a dearth in this revolting land.
    Or shall we play the wantons with our woes
    And make some pretty match with shedding tears ?   165
    As thus : to drop them still upon one place
    Till they have fretted us a pair of graves
    Within the earth ; and, therein laid—there lies
    Two kinsmen digg'd their graves with weeping eyes.
    Would not this ill do well ?   Well, well, I see   170
    I talk but idly, and you laugh at me.
    Most mighty prince, my Lord Northumberland,
    What says King Bolingbroke ?   Will his Majesty
    Give Richard leave to live till Richard die ?
    You make a leg, and Bolingbroke says ay.   175
NORTH. My lord, in the base court he doth attend
    To speak with you ; may it please you to come down ?
K. RICH. Down, down I come, like glist'ring Phaethon,
    Wanting the manage of unruly jades.
    In the base court ?   Base court, where kings grow base,   180
    To come at traitors' calls, and do them grace.
    In the base court ?   Come down ?   Down, court ! down, king !
    For night-owls shriek where mounting larks should sing.
                                        [*Exeunt from above.*

BOLING. What says his Majesty ?
NORTH.   Sorrow and grief of heart
   Makes him speak fondly, like a frantic man ;   185
   Yet he is come.

       Enter the KING, *and his* Attendants, *below.*

BOLING. Stand all apart,
   And show fair duty to his Majesty.   [*He kneels down.*
   My gracious lord—
K. RICH. Fair cousin, you debase your princely knee   190
   To make the base earth proud with kissing it.
   Me rather had my heart might feel your love
   Than my unpleas'd eye see your courtesy.
   Up, cousin, up ; your heart is up, I know,
   [*Touching his own head.*] Thus high at least, although your knee
      be low.   195
BOLING. My gracious lord, I come but for mine own.
K. RICH. Your own is yours, and I am yours, and all.
BOLING. So far be mine, my most redoubted lord,
   As my true service shall deserve your love.
K. RICH. Well you deserve. They well deserve to have   200
   That know the strong'st and surest way to get.
   Uncle, give me your hands ; nay, dry your eyes :
   Tears show their love, but want their remedies.
   Cousin, I am too young to be your father,
   Though you are old enough to be my heir.   205
   What you will have, I'll give, and willing too ;
   For do we must what force will have us do.
   Set on towards London. Cousin, is it so ?
BOLING. Yea, my good lord.
K. RICH.   Then I must not say no.
                          [*Flourish. Exeunt.*

      SCENE IV. *The Duke of York's garden.*

        Enter the QUEEN *and two* Ladies.

SCENE 15
Exterior. The Duke of
York's Garden. Day.

QUEEN. What sport shall we devise here in this garden
   To drive away the heavy thought of care ?
LADY. Madam, we'll play at bowls.
QUEEN. 'Twill make me think the world is full of rubs
   And that my fortune runs against the bias.   5
LADY. Madam, we'll dance.
QUEEN. My legs can keep no measure in delight,
   When my poor heart no measure keeps in grief ;
   Therefore no dancing, girl ; some other sport.
LADY. Madam, we'll tell tales.   10
QUEEN. Of sorrow or of joy ?
LADY.   Of either, madam.
QUEEN. Of neither, girl ;
   For if of joy, being altogether wanting,
   It doth remember me the more of sorrow
   Or if of grief, being altogether had,   15
   It adds more sorrow to my want of joy ;
   For what I have I need not to repeat,

And what I want it boots not to complain.
LADY. Madam, I'll sing.
QUEEN.   'Tis well that thou hast cause ;
  But thou shouldst please me better wouldst thou weep.   20
LADY. I could weep, madam, would it do you good.
QUEEN. And I could sing, would weeping do me good,
  And never borrow any tear of thee.

      Enter a Gardener *and two* Servants.

But stay, here come the gardeners.
  Let's step into the shadow of these trees.   25
  My wretchedness unto a row of pins,
  They will talk of state, for every one doth so
  Against a change : woe is forerun with woe.
                          [QUEEN *and* Ladies *retire.*
GARD. Go, bind thou up yon dangling apricocks,
  Which, like unruly children make their sire   30
  Stoop with oppression of their prodigal weight ;
  Give some supportance to the bending twigs.
  Go thou, and like an executioner
  Cut off the heads of too fast growing sprays
  That look too lofty in our commonwealth :   35
  All must be even in our government.
  You thus employ'd, I will go root away
  The noisome weeds which without profit suck
  The soil's fertility from wholesome flowers.
SERV. Why should we, in the compass of a pale,   40
  Keep law and form and due proportion,
  Showing, as in a model, our firm estate,
  When our sea-walled garden, the whole land,
  Is full of weeds ; her fairest flowers chok'd up,
  Her fruit trees all unprun'd, her hedges ruin'd,   45
  Her knots disordered, and her wholesome herbs
  Swarming with caterpillars ?
GARD.   Hold thy peace.
  He that hath suffer'd this disorder'd spring
  Hath now himself met with the fall of leaf ;
  The weeds which his broad-spreading leaves did shelter,   50
  That seem'd in eating him to hold him up,
  Are pluck'd up root and all by Bolingbroke—
  I mean the Earl of Wiltshire, Bushy, Green.
SERV. What, are they dead ?
GARD.   They are ; and Bolingbroke
  Hath seiz'd the wasteful king. O, what pity is it   55
  That he had not so trimm'd and dress'd his land
  As we this garden ! We at time of year
  Do wound the bark, the skin of our fruit trees,
  Lest, being over-proud in sap and blood,
  With too much riches it confound itself ;   60
  Had he done so to great and growing men,
  They might have liv'd to bear, and he to taste
  Their fruits of duty. Superfluous branches
  We lop away, that bearing boughs may live ;
  Had he done so, himself had borne the crown   65

                                   Lines 55 from 'O,
                                   what pity' to 71
                                   omitted.

Which waste of idle hours hath quite thrown down.   Lines 55–71 omitted.
SERV. What, think you the King shall be deposed ?
GARD. Depress'd he is already, and depos'd
'Tis doubt he will be.   Letters came last night
To a dear friend of the good Duke of York's   70
That tell black tidings.
QUEEN. O, I am press'd to death through want of speaking !
                              [*Coming forward.*
Thou, old Adam's likeness, set to dress this garden,
How dares thy harsh rude tongue sound this unpleasing news ?
What Eve, what serpent, hath suggested thee   75
To make a second fall of cursed man ?
Why dost thou say King Richard is depos'd ?
Dar'st thou, thou little better thing than earth,
Divine his downfall ?   Say, where, when, and how,
Cam'st thou by this ill tidings ?   Speak, thou wretch.   80
GARD. Pardon me, madam ; little joy have I
To breathe this news ; yet what I say is true.
King Richard, he is in the mighty hold
Of Bolingbroke.   Their fortunes both are weigh'd.
In your lord's scale is nothing but himself,   85
And some few vanities that make him light ;
But in the balance of great Bolingbroke,
Besides himself, are all the English peers,
And with that odds he weighs King Richard down.
Post you to London, and you will find it so ;   90
I speak no more than every one doth know.
QUEEN. Nimble mischance, that art so light of foot,
Doth not thy embassage belong to me,
And am I last that knows it ?   O, thou thinkest
To serve me last, that I may longest keep   95
Thy sorrow in my breast.   Come, ladies, go
To meet at London London's king in woe.
What, was I born to this, that my sad look
Should grace the triumph of great Bolingbroke ?
Gard'ner, for telling me these news of woe,   100
Pray God the plants thou graft'st may never grow !
                         [*Exeunt* QUEEN *and* Ladies.   All *exeunt.*
GARD. Poor Queen, so that thy state might be no worse,   Lines 102–107
I would my skill were subject to thy curse.   omitted.
Here did she fall a tear ; here in this place
I'll set a bank of rue, sour herb of grace.   105
Rue, even for ruth, here shortly shall be seen,
In the remembrance of a weeping queen.   [*Exeunt.*

ACT FOUR

SCENE I. *Westminster Hall.*

Enter, as to the Parliament, BOLINGBROKE, AUMERLE, NORTHUMBER-
LAND, PERCY, FITZWATER, SURREY, *the* BISHOP OF CARLISLE, *the*
ABBOT OF WESTMINSTER, *and* Others ; Herald, Officers, and
BAGOT.

BOLING. Call forth Bagot.
   Now, Bagot, freely speak thy mind—   Lines 1–106 omitted.
   What thou dost know of noble Gloucester's death ;
   Who wrought it with the King, and who perform'd
   The bloody office of his timeless end.   5
BAGOT. Then set before my face the Lord Aumerle.
BOLING. Cousin, stand forth, and look upon that man.
BAGOT. My Lord Aumerle, I know your daring tongue
   Scorns to unsay what once it hath deliver'd.
   In that dead time when Gloucester's death was plotted   10
   I heard you say ' Is not my arm of length,
   That reacheth from the restful English Court
   As far as Calais, to mine uncle's head ? '
   Amongst much other talk that very time
   I heard you say that you had rather refuse   15
   The offer of an hundred thousand crowns
   Than Bolingbroke's return to England ;
   Adding withal, how blest this land would be
   In this your cousin's death.
AUM. Princes, and noble lords,
   What answer shall I make to this base man ?   20
   Shall I so much dishonour my fair stars
   On equal terms to give him chastisement ?
   Either I must, or have mine honour soil'd
   With the attainder of his slanderous lips.
   There is my gage, the manual seal of death   25
   That marks thee out for hell.   I say thou liest,
   And will maintain what thou hast said is false
   In thy heart-blood, though being all too base
   To stain the temper of my knightly sword.
BOLING. Bagot, forbear ; thou shalt not take it up.   30
AUM. Excepting one, I would he were the best
   In all this presence that hath mov'd me so.
FITZ. If that thy valour stand on sympathy,
   There is my gage, Aumerle, in gage to thine.
   By that fair sun which shows me where thou stand'st,   35
   I heard thee say, and vauntingly thou spak'st it,
   That thou wert cause of noble Gloucester's death.
   If thou deniest it twenty times, thou liest ;
   And I will turn thy falsehood to thy heart,
   Where it was forged, with my rapier's point.   40
AUM. Thou dar'st not, coward, live to see that day.
FITZ. Now, by my soul, I would it were this hour.
AUM. Fitzwater, thou art damn'd to hell for this.
PERCY. Aumerle, thou liest ; his honour is as true

In this appeal as thou art all unjust ;   45
And that thou art so, there I throw my gage,
To prove it on thee to the extremest point
Of mortal breathing.   Seize it, if thou dar'st.
AUM. An if I do not, may my hands rot off
And never brandish more revengeful steel   50
Over the glittering helmet of my foe !
ANOTHER LORD. I task the earth to the like, forsworn Aumerle ;
And spur thee on with full as many lies
As may be halloa'd in thy treacherous ear
From sun to sun.   There is my honour's pawn ;   55
Engage it to the trial, if thou darest.
AUM. Who sets me else ?   By heaven, I'll throw at all !
I have a thousand spirits in one breast
To answer twenty thousand such as you.
SURREY. My Lord Fitzwater, I do remember well   60
The very time Aumerle and you did talk.
FITZ. 'Tis very true ; you were in presence then,
And you can witness with me this is true.
SURREY. As false, by heaven, as heaven itself is true.
FITZ. Surrey, thou liest.
SURREY.   Dishonourable boy !   65
That lie shall lie so heavy on my sword
That it shall render vengeance and revenge
Till thou the lie-giver and that lie do lie
In earth as quiet as thy father's skull.
In proof whereof, there is my honour's pawn ;   70
Engage it to the trial, if thou dar'st.
FITZ. How fondly dost thou spur a forward horse !
If I dare eat, or drink, or breathe, or live,
I dare meet Surrey in a wilderness,
And spit upon him whilst I say he lies,   75
And lies, and lies.   There is my bond of faith,
To tie thee to my strong correction.
As I intend to thrive in this new world,
Aumerle is guilty of my true appeal.
Besides, I heard the banish'd Norfolk say   80
That thou, Aumerle, didst send two of thy men
To execute the noble Duke at Calais.
AUM. Some honest Christian trust me with a gage
That Norfolk lies.   Here do I throw down this,
If he may be repeal'd to try his honour.   85
BOLING. These differences shall all rest under gage
Till Norfolk be repeal'd—repeal'd he shall be
And, though mine enemy, restor'd again
To all his lands and signories.   When he is return'd,
Against Aumerle we will enforce his trial.   90
CAR. That honourable day shall never be seen.
Many a time hath banish'd Norfolk fought
For Jesu Christ in glorious Christian field,
Streaming the ensign of the Christian cross
Against black pagans, Turks, and Saracens ;   95
And, toil'd with works of war, retir'd himself
To Italy ; and there, at Venice, gave

This page omitted.

His body to that pleasant country's earth,
And his pure soul unto his captain, Christ,
Under whose colours he had fought so long.   100
BOLING. Why, Bishop, is Norfolk dead?
CAR. As surely as I live, my lord.
BOLING. Sweet peace conduct his sweet soul to the bosom
  Of good old Abraham!   Lords appellants,
  Your differences shall all rest under gage   105
  Till we assign you to your days of trial.

Lines 1–106 omitted.

Enter YORK, *attended.*

SCENE 16
*Interior. Westminster
Hall. Day.*
BOLINGBROKE,
AUMERLE,
NORTHUMBERLAND,
PERCY, FITZWATER,
SURREY, BISHOP OF
CARLISLE, ABBOT OF
WESTMINSTER,
BAGOT.
Enter YORK *alone.*

YORK. Great Duke of Lancaster, I come to thee
  From plume-pluck'd Richard, who with willing soul
  Adopts thee heir, and his high sceptre yields
  To the possession of thy royal hand.   110
  Ascend his throne, descending now from him—
  And long live Henry, fourth of that name!
BOLING. In God's name, I'll ascend the regal throne.
CAR. Marry, God forbid!
  Worst in this royal presence may I speak,   115
  Yet best beseeming me to speak the truth.
  Would God that any in this noble presence
  Were enough noble to be upright judge
  Of noble Richard!   Then true noblesse would
  Learn him forbearance from so foul a wrong.   120
  What subject can give sentence on his king?
  And who sits here that is not Richard's subject?
  Thieves are not judg'd but they are by to hear,
  Although apparent guilt be seen in them;
  And shall the figure of God's majesty,   125
  His captain, steward, deputy elect,
  Anointed, crowned, planted many years,
  Be judg'd by subject and inferior breath,
  And he himself not present?   O, forfend it, God,
  That in a Christian climate souls refin'd   130
  Should show so heinous, black, obscene a deed!
  I speak to subjects, and a subject speaks,
  Stirr'd up by God, thus boldly for his king.
  My Lord of Hereford here, whom you call king,
  Is a foul traitor to proud Hereford's king;   135
  And if you crown him, let me prophesy—
  The blood of English shall manure the ground,
  And future ages groan for this foul act;
  Peace shall go sleep with Turks and infidels,
  And in this seat of peace tumultuous wars   140
  Shall kin with kin and kind with kind confound;
  Disorder, horror, fear, and mutiny,
  Shall here inhabit, and this land be call'd
  The field of Golgotha and dead men's skulls.
  O, if you raise this house against this house,   145
  It will the woefullest division prove
  That ever fell upon this cursed earth.
  Prevent it, resist it, let it not be so,
  Lest child, child's children, cry against you woe.

72

NORTH. Well have you argued, sir ; and, for your pains,   150
  Of capital treason we arrest you here.
  My Lord of Westminster, be it your charge
  To keep him safely till his day of trial.
  May it please you, lords, to grant the commons' suit ?
BOLING. Fetch hither Richard, that in common view   155
  He may surrender ; so we shall proceed
  Without suspicion.
YORK.   I will be his conduct.   [*Exit.*
BOLING. Lords, you that here are under our arrest,   Lines 158–161
  Procure your sureties for your days of answer.   omitted.
  Little are we beholding to your love,   160
  And little look'd for at your helping hands.

Re-enter YORK, *with* KING RICHARD, *and* Officers *bearing the regalia.*

K. RICH. Alack, why am I sent for to a king,
  Before I have shook off the regal thoughts
  Wherewith I reign'd ?   I hardly yet have learn'd
  To insinuate, flatter, bow, and bend my knee.   165
  Give sorrow leave awhile to tutor me
  To this submission.   Yet I well remember
  The favours of these men.   Were they not mine ?
  Did they not sometime cry ' All hail ! ' to me ?
  So Judas did to Christ ; but he, in twelve,   170
  Found truth in all but one ; I, in twelve thousand, none.
  God save the King !   Will no man say amen ?
  Am I both priest and clerk ?   Well then, amen.
  God save the King ! although I be not he ;
  And yet, amen, if heaven do think him me.   175
  To do what service am I sent for hither ?
YORK. To do that office of thine own good will
  Which tired majesty did make thee offer—
  The resignation of thy state and crown
  To Henry Bolingbroke.   180
K. RICH. Give me the crown.   Here, cousin, seize the crown.
  Here, cousin,
  On this side my hand, and on that side thine.
  Now is this golden crown like a deep well
  That owes two buckets, filling one another ;   185
  The emptier ever dancing in the air,
  The other down, unseen, and full of water.
  That bucket down and full of tears am I,
  Drinking my griefs, whilst you mount up on high.
BOLING. I thought you had been willing to resign.   190
K. RICH. My crown I am ; but still my griefs are mine.
  You may my glories and my state depose,
  But not my griefs ; still am I king of those.
BOLING. Part of your cares you give me with your crown.
K. RICH. Your cares set up do not pluck my cares down.   195
  My care is loss of care, by old care done ;
  Your care is gain of care, by new care won.
  The cares I give I have, though given away ;
  They tend the crown, yet still with me they stay.
BOLING. Are you contented to resign the crown ?   200

K. RICH. Ay, no ; no, ay ; for I must nothing be ;
  Therefore no no, for I resign to thee.
  Now mark me how I will undo myself :
  I give this heavy weight from off my head,
  And this unwieldy sceptre from my hand,   205
  The pride of kingly sway from out my heart ;
  With mine own tears I wash away my balm,
  With mine own hands I give away my crown,
  With mine own tongue deny my sacred state,
  With mine own breath release all duteous oaths ;   210
  All pomp and majesty I do forswear ;
  My manors, rents, revenues, I forgo ;
  My acts, decrees, and statutes, I deny.
  God pardon all oaths that are broke to me !
  God keep all vows unbroke are made to thee !   215
  Make me, that nothing have, with nothing griev'd,
  And thou with all pleas'd, that hast all achiev'd.
  Long mayst thou live in Richard's seat to sit,
  And soon lie Richard in an earthy pit.
  God save King Henry, unking'd Richard says,   220
  And send him many years of sunshine days !
  What more remains ?
NORTH.   No more ; but that you read
  These accusations, and these grievous crimes
  Committed by your person and your followers
  Against the state and profit of this land ;   225
  That, by confessing them, the souls of men
  May deem that you are worthily depos'd.
K. RICH. Must I do so ? And must I ravel out
  My weav'd-up follies ? Gentle Northumberland,
  If thy offences were upon record,   230
  Would it not shame thee in so fair a troop
  To read a lecture of them ? If thou wouldst,
  There shouldst thou find one heinous article,
  Containing the deposing of a king
  And cracking the strong warrant of an oath,   235
  Mark'd with a blot, damn'd in the book of heaven.
  Nay, all of you that stand and look upon me
  Whilst that my wretchedness doth bait myself,
  Though some of you, with Pilate, wash your hands,
  Showing an outward pity—yet you Pilates   240
  Have here deliver'd me to my sour cross,
  And water cannot wash away your sin.
NORTH. My lord, dispatch ; read o'er these articles.
K. RICH. Mine eyes are full of tears ; I cannot see.
  And yet salt water blinds them not so much   245
  But they can see a sort of traitors here.
  Nay, if I turn mine eyes upon myself,
  I find myself a traitor with the rest ;
  For I have given here my soul's consent
  T'undeck the pompous body of a king ;   250
  Made glory base, and sovereignty a slave,
  Proud majesty a subject, state a peasant.
NORTH. My lord—

K. RICH. No lord of thine, thou haught insulting man,
  Nor no man's lord ; I have no name, no title—   255
  No, not that name was given me at the font—
  But 'tis usurp'd.   Alack the heavy day,
  That I have worn so many winters out,
  And know not now what name to call myself !
  O that I were a mockery king of snow,   260
  Standing before the sun of Bolingbroke
  To melt myself away in water drops !
  Good king, great king, and yet not greatly good,
  An if my word be sterling yet in England,
  Let it command a mirror hither straight,   265
  That it may show me what a face I have
  Since it is bankrupt of his majesty.
BOLING. Go some of you and fetch a looking-glass.
                                      [*Exit an* Attendant.
NORTH. Read o'er this paper while the glass doth come.
K. RICH. Fiend, thou torments me ere I come to hell.   270
BOLING. Urge it no more, my Lord Northumberland.
NORTH. The Commons will not, then, be satisfied.
K. RICH. They shall be satisfied.   I'll read enough,
  When I do see the very book indeed
  Where all my sins are writ, and that's myself.   275

           Re-enter Attendant *with glass.*

  Give me that glass, and therein will I read.
  No deeper wrinkles yet ?   Hath sorrow struck
  So many blows upon this face of mine
  And made no deeper wounds ?   O flatt'ring glass,
  Like to my followers in prosperity,   280
  Thou dost beguile me !   Was this face the face
  That every day under his household roof
  Did keep ten thousand men ?   Was this the face
  That like the sun did make beholders wink ?
  Is this the face which fac'd so many follies   285
  That was at last out-fac'd by Bolingbroke ?
  A brittle glory shineth in this face ;
  As brittle as the glory is the face ;
                  [*Dashes the glass against the ground.*
  For there it is, crack'd in a hundred shivers.
  Mark, silent king, the moral of this sport—   290
  How soon my sorrow hath destroy'd my face.
BOLING. The shadow of your sorrow hath destroy'd
  The shadow of your face.
K. RICH.   Say that again.
  The shadow of my sorrow ?   Ha ! let's see.
  'Tis very true : my grief lies all within ;   295
  And these external manner of laments
  Are merely shadows to the unseen grief
  That swells with silence in the tortur'd soul.
  There lies the substance ; and I thank thee, king,
  For thy great bounty, that not only giv'st   300
  Me cause to wail, but teachest me the way
  How to lament the cause.   I'll beg one boon,

And then be gone and trouble you no more.
Shall I obtain it?
BOLING.   Name it, fair cousin.
K. RICH. Fair cousin! I am greater than a king;   305
For when I was a king, my flatterers
Were then but subjects; being now a subject,
I have a king here to my flatterer.
Being so great, I have no need to beg.
BOLING. Yet ask.   310
K. RICH. And shall I have?
BOLING. You shall.
X. RICH. Then give me leave to go.
BOLING. Whither?
K. RICH. Whither you will, so I were from your sights.   315
BOLING. Go, some of you convey him to the Tower.
K. RICH. O, Good! Convey! Conveyers are you all,
That rise thus nimbly by a true king's fall.
              [*Exeunt* KING RICHARD, *some* Lords *and a* Guard.
BOLING. On Wednesday next we solemnly set down
Our coronation. Lords, prepare yourselves.   320
        [*Exeunt all but the* ABBOT OF WESTMINSTER, *the* BISHOP OF
                                    CARLISLE, *and* AUMERLE.
ABBOT. A woeful pageant have we here beheld.
CAR. The woe's to come; the children yet unborn
Shall feel this day as sharp to them as thorn.
AUM. You holy clergymen, is there no plot
To rid the realm of this pernicious blot?   325
ABBOT. My lord,
Before I freely speak my mind herein,
You shall not only take the sacrament
To bury mine intents, but also to effect
Whatever I shall happen to devise.   330
I see your brows are full of discontent,
Your hearts of sorrow, and your eyes of tears.
Come home with me to supper; I will lay
A plot shall show us all a merry day.   [*Exeunt.*

ACT FIVE

SCENE I. London. *A street leading to the Tower.*
Enter the QUEEN, *with her* Attendants.

QUEEN. This way the King will come; this is the way
To Julius Cæsar's ill-erected tower,
To whose flint bosom my condemned lord
Is doom'd a prisoner by proud Bolingbroke.
Here let us rest, if this rebellious earth   5
Have any resting for her true king's queen.

Enter KING RICHARD *and* Guard.

But soft, but see, or rather do not see,
My fair rose wither. Yet look up, behold,
That you in pity may dissolve to dew,
And wash him fresh again with true-love tears.   10

SCENE 17
*Interior. A Corridor in
the Palace of
Westminster. Day.*
ABBOT OF
WESTMINSTER,
AUMERLE, BISHOP OF
CARLISLE.

Lines 326–334
omitted.

SCENE 18
*Exterior. London.
A Street. Night.*

Ah, thou, the model where old Troy did stand ;
Thou map of honour, thou King Richard's tomb,
And not King Richard ; thou most beauteous inn,
Why should hard-favour'd grief be lodg'd in thee,
When triumph is become an alehouse guest ?   15
K. RICH. Join not with grief, fair woman, do not so,
To make my end too sudden.   Learn, good soul,
To think our former state a happy dream ;
From which awak'd, the truth of what we are
Shows us but this : I am sworn brother, sweet,   20
To grim Necessity ; and he and I
Will keep a league till death.   Hie thee to France,
And cloister thee in some religious house.
Our holy lives must win a new world's crown,
Which our profane hours here have thrown down.   25
QUEEN. What, is my Richard both in shape and mind
Transform'd and weak'ned ?   Hath Bolingbroke depos'd
Thine intellect ?   Hath he been in thy heart ?
The lion dying thrusteth forth his paw
And wounds the earth, if nothing else, with rage   30
To be o'erpow'r'd ; and wilt thou, pupil-like,
Take the correction mildly, kiss the rod,
And fawn on rage with base humility,
Which art a lion and the king of beasts ?
K. RICH. A king of beasts, indeed !   If aught but beasts,   35
I had been still a happy king of men.
Good sometimes queen, prepare thee hence for France.
Think I am dead, and that even here thou takest,
As from my death-bed, thy last living leave.
In winter's tedious nights sit by the fire   40
With good old folks, and let them tell thee tales
Of woeful ages long ago betid ;
And ere thou bid good night, to quit their griefs
Tell thou the lamentable tale of me,
And send the hearers weeping to their beds ;   45
For why the senseless brands will sympathize
The heavy accent of thy moving tongue,
And in compassion weep the fire out ;
And some will mourn in ashes, some coal-black,
For the deposing of a rightful king.   50

          Enter NORTHUMBERLAND *attended.*

NORTH. My lord, the mind of Bolingbroke is chang'd
You must to Pomfret, not unto the Tower.
And, madam, there is order ta'en for you :
With all swift speed you must away to France
K. RICH. Northumberland, thou ladder wherewithal   55
The mounting Bolingbroke ascends my throne,
The time shall not be many hours of age
More than it is, ere foul sin gathering head
Shall break into corruption.   Thou shalt think
Though he divide the realm and give thee half   60
It is too little, helping him to all ;
And he shall think that thou, which knowest the way

To plant unrightful kings, wilt know again,
Being ne'er so little urg'd, another way
To pluck him headlong from the usurped throne.   65
The love of wicked men converts to fear ;
That fear to hate ; and hate turns one or both
To worthy danger and deserved death.

NORTH. My guilt be on my head, and there an end.
Take leave, and part ; for you must part forthwith.   70

K. RICH. Doubly divorc'd ! Bad men, you violate
A twofold marriage—'twixt my crown and me,
And then betwixt me and my married wife.
Let me unkiss the oath 'twixt thee and me ;
And yet not so, for with a kiss 'twas made.   75
Part us, Northumberland ; I towards the north,
Where shivering cold and sickness pines the clime ;
My wife to France, from whence set forth in pomp,
She came adorned hither like sweet May,
Sent back like Hallowmas or short'st of day.   80

QUEEN. And must we be divided ? Must we part ?

K. RICH. Ay, hand from hand, my love, and heart from heart.

QUEEN. Banish us both, and send the King with me.

NORTH. That were some love, but little policy.

QUEEN. Then whither he goes thither let me go.   85

K. RICH. So two, together weeping, make one woe.
Weep thou for me in France, I for thee here ;
Better far off than near, be ne'er the near.
Go, count thy way with sighs ; I mine with groans.

QUEEN. So longest way shall have the longest moans.   90

K. RICH. Twice for one step I'll groan, the way being short,
And piece the way out with a heavy heart.
Come, come, in wooing sorrow let's be brief,
Since, wedding it, there is such length in grief.
One kiss shall stop our mouths, and dumbly part ;   95
Thus give I mine, and thus take I thy heart.

QUEEN. Give me mine own again ; 'twere no good part
To take on me to keep and kill thy heart.
So, now I have mine own again, be gone.
That I may strive to kill it with a groan.   100

K. RICH. We make woe wanton with this fond delay.
Once more, adieu ; the rest let sorrow say.   [*Exeunt.*

SCENE II.   *The* DUKE OF YORK'S *palace.*

Enter the DUKE OF YORK *and the* DUCHESS.

SCENE 19
*Interior. The Duke of
York's House. Day.*

DUCH. My Lord, you told me you would tell the rest,
When weeping made you break the story off,
Of our two cousins' coming into London.

YORK. Where did I leave ?

DUCH.   At that sad stop, my lord,
Where rude misgoverned hands from windows' tops   5
Threw dust and rubbish on King Richard's head.

YORK. Then, as I said, the Duke, great Bolingbroke,
Mounted upon a hot and fiery steed
Which his aspiring rider seem'd to know,

With slow but stately pace kept on his course,   10
Whilst all tongues cried ' God save thee, Bolingbroke ! '
You would have thought the very windows spake,
So many greedy looks of young and old
Through casements darted their desiring eyes
Upon his visage ; and that all the walls   15
With painted imagery had said at once
' Jesu preserve thee !   Welcome, Bolingbroke !'
Whilst he, from the one side to the other turning,
Bareheaded, lower than his proud steed's neck,
Bespake them thus, 'I thank you, countrymen '.   20
And thus still doing, thus he pass'd along.
DUCH. Alack, poor Richard ! where rode he the whilst ?
YORK. As in a theatre the eyes of men
After a well-grac'd actor leaves the stage
Are idly bent on him that enters next,   25
Thinking his prattle to be tedious ;
Even so, or with much more contempt, men's eyes
Did scowl on gentle Richard ; no man cried ' God save him ! '
No joyful tongue gave him his welcome home ;
But dust was thrown upon his sacred head ;   30
Which with such gentle sorrow he shook off,
His face still combating with tears and smiles,
The badges of his grief and patience,
That had not God, for some strong purpose, steel'd
The hearts of men, they must perforce have melted,   35
And barbarism itself have pitied him.
But heaven hath a hand in these events,
To whose high will we bound our calm contents.
To Bolingbroke are we sworn subjects now,
Whose state and honour I for aye allow.   40
DUCH. Here comes my son Aumerle.
YORK.   Aumerle that was
But that is lost for being Richard's friend,
And madam, you must call him Rutland now.
I am in Parliament pledge for his truth
And lasting fealty to the new-made king.   45

Enter AUMERLE.

DUCH. Welcome, my son.   Who are the violets now
That strew the green lap of the new come spring ?
AUM. Madame, I know not, nor I greatly care not.
God knows I had as lief be none as one.
YORK. Well, bear you well in this new spring of time,   50
Lest you be cropp'd before you come to prime.
What news from Oxford ?   Do these justs and triumphs hold ?
AUM. For aught I know, my lord, they do.
YORK. You will be there, I know.
AUM. If God prevent not, I purpose so.   55
YORK. What seal is that that hangs without thy bosom ?
Yea, look'st thou pale ?   Let me see the writing.
AUM. My lord, 'tis nothing.
YORK.   No matter, then, who see it.
I will be satisfied ; let me see the writing.

79

AUM. I do beseech your Grace to pardon me;   60
    It is a matter of small consequence
    Which for some reasons I would not have seen.
YORK. Which for some reasons, sir, I mean to see.
    I fear, I fear—
DUCH.   What should you fear?
    'Tis nothing but some bond that he is ent'red into   65
    For gay apparel 'gainst the triumph-day.
YORK. Bound to himself! What doth he with a bond
    That he is bound to? Wife, thou art a fool.
    Boy, let me see the writing.
AUM. I do beseech you, pardon me; I may not show it.   70
YORK. I will be satisfied; let me see it, I say. [*He plucks it out of*
                                   his bosom, and reads it.
    Treason, foul treason! Villain! traitor! slave!
DUCH. What is the matter, my lord?
YORK. Ho! who is within there?

               Enter a Servant.

               Saddle my horse.
    God for his mercy, what treachery is here!   75
DUCH. Why, what is it, my lord?
YORK. Give me my boots, I say; saddle my horse. [*Exit* Servant.
    Now, by mine honour, by my life, my troth,
    I will appeach the villain.
DUCH.   What is the matter?
YORK. Peace, foolish woman.   80
DUCH. I will not peace. What is the matter, Aumerle?
AUM. Good mother, be content; it is no more
    Than my poor life must answer.
DUCH.   Thy life answer!
YORK. Bring me my boots. I will unto the King.

         His Man *enters with his boots.*

DUCH. Strike him, Aumerle. Poor boy, thou art amaz'd.   85
    Hence, villain! never more come in my sight.
YORK. Give me my boots, I say.
DUCH. Why, York, what wilt thou do?
    Wilt thou not hide the trespass of thine own?
    Have we more sons? or are we like to have?   90
    Is not my teeming date drunk up with time?
    And wilt thou pluck my fair son from mine age
    And rob me of a happy mother's name?
    Is he not like thee? Is he not thine own?
YORK. Thou fond mad woman,   95
    Wilt thou conceal this dark conspiracy?
    A dozen of them here have ta'en the sacrament,
    And interchangeably set down their hands
    To kill the King at Oxford.
DUCH.   He shall be none;
    We'll keep him here. Then what is that to him?   100
YORK. Away fond woman! were he twenty times my son
    I would appeach him.
DUCH.   Hadst thou groan'd for him

As I have done, thou wouldst be more pitiful.
But now I know thy mind : thou dost suspect
That I have been disloyal to thy bed   105
And that he is a bastard, not thy son.
Sweet York, sweet husband, be not of that mind.
He is as like thee as a man may be,
Not like to me, or any of my kin,
And yet I love him.
YORK.   Make way, unruly woman !   [*Exit.*
DUCH. Aftèr, Aumerle !   Mount thee upon his horse ;
Spur post, and get before him to the King,
And beg thy pardon ere he do accuse thee.
I'll not be long behind ; though I be old,
I doubt not but to ride as fast as York ;   115
And never will I rise up from the ground
Till Bolingbroke have pardon'd thee.   Away, be gone.   [*Exeunt.*

SCENE III.   *Windsor Castle.*

Enter BOLINGBROKE *as King,* PERCY, *and other* Lords.

BOLING. Can no man tell me of my unthrifty son ?   Lines 1–23 omitted.
'Tis full three months since I did see him last.
If any plague hang over us, 'tis he.
I would :o God, my lords, he might be found.
Inquire at London, 'mongst the taverns there,   5
For there, they say, he daily doth frequent
With unrestrained loose companions,
Even such, they say, as stand in narrow lanes
And beat our watch and rob our passengers,
Which he, young wanton and effeminate boy,   10
Takes on the point of honour to support
So dissolute a crew.
PERCY. My lord, some two days since I saw the Prince,
And told him of those triumphs held at Oxford.
BOLING. And what said the gallant ?   15
PERCY. His answer was, he would unto the stews,
And from the common'st creature pluck a glove
And wear it as a favour ; and with that
He would unhorse the lustiest challenger.
BOLING. As dissolute as desperate ; yet through both   20
I see some sparks of better hope, which elder years
May happily bring forth.   But who comes here ?

Enter AUMERLE *amazed.*

AUM. Where is the King ?
BOLING. What means our cousin that he stares and looks   SCENE 20
So wildly ?   25   *Interior. Windsor*
AUM. God save your Grace !   I do beseech your Majesty,   *Castle. The King's*
To have some conference with your Grace alone.   *Chambers. Day.*
BOLING. Withdraw yourselves, and leave us here alone.   BOLINGBROKE,
                       [*Exeunt* PERCY *and* Lords.   PERCY, AUMERLE and
What is the matter with our cousin now ?   other Lords.
AUM. For ever may my knees grow to the earth,   [*Kneels.*
My tongue cleave to my roof within my mouth,

Unless a pardon ere I rise or speak.
BOLING. Intended or committed was this fault ?
    If on the first, how heinous e'er it be,
    To win thy after-love I pardon thee.   35
AUM. Then give me leave that I may turn the key,
    That no man enter till my tale be done.
BOLING. Have thy desire.   [*The* DUKE OF YORK *knocks at the door and*
                                                          crieth.
YORK. [*Within.*]   My liege, beware ; look to thyself ;
    Thou hast a traitor in thy presence there.   40
BOLING. [*Drawing.*]   Villain, I'll make thee safe.
AUM. Stay thy revengeful hand ; thou hast no cause to fear.
YORK. [*Within.*]   Open the door, secure, foolhardy King.
    Shall I, for love, speak treason to thy face ?
    Open the door, or I will break it open.   45

Enter YORK.

BOLING. What is the matter, uncle ?   Speak ;
    Recover breath ; tell us how near is danger,
    That we may arm us to encounter it.
YORK. Peruse this writing here, and thou shalt know
    The treason that my haste forbids me show.   50
AUM. Remember, as thou read'st, thy promise pass'd.
    I do repent me ; read not my name there ;
    My heart is not confederate with my hand.
YORK. It was, villain, ere thy hand did set it down.
    I tore it from the traitor's bosom, King ;   55
    Fear, and not love, begets his penitence.
    Forget to pity him, lest thy pity prove
    A serpent that will sting thee to the heart.
BOLING. O heinous, strong, and bold conspiracy !
    O loyal father of a treacherous son !   60
    Thou sheer, immaculate, and silver fountain,
    From whence this stream through muddy passages
    Hath held his current and defil'd himself !
    Thy overflow of good converts to bad ;
    And thy abundant goodness shall excuse   65
    This deadly blot in thy digressing son.
YORK. So shall my virtue be his vice's bawd ;
    And he shall spend mine honour with his shame,
    As thriftless sons their scraping fathers' gold.
    Mine honour lives when his dishonour dies,   70
    Or my sham'd life in his dishonour lies.
    Thou kill'st me in his life ; giving him breath,
    The traitor lives, the true man's put to death.
DUCH. [*Within.*]   What ho, my liege, for God's sake, let me in.
BOLING. What shrill-voic'd suppliant makes this eager cry ?   75
DUCH. [*Within.*]   A woman, and thine aunt, great King ; 'tis I.
    Speak with me, pity me, open the door.
    A beggar begs that never begg'd before.
BOLING. Our scene is alt'red from a serious thing,
    And now chang'd to ' The Beggar and the King '.   80
    My dangerous cousin, let your mother in.
    I know she is come to pray for your foul sin.

YORK. If thou do pardon whosoever pray,
  More sins for this forgiveness prosper may.
  This fest'red joint cut off, the rest rest sound ;   85
  This let alone will all the rest confound.

                    Enter DUCHESS.

DUCH. O King, believe not this hard-hearted man !
  Love loving not itself, none other can.
YORK. Thou frantic woman, what dost thou make here ?
  Shall thy old dugs once more a traitor rear ?   90
DUCH. Sweet York, be patient. Hear me, gentle liege. [*Kneels.*
BOLING. Rise up, good aunt.
DUCH.   Not yet, I thee beseech.
  For ever will I walk upon my knees,
  And never see day that the happy sees
  Till thou give joy ; until thou bid me joy   95
  By pardoning Rutland, my transgressing boy.
AUM. Unto my mother's prayers I bend my knee.   [*Kneels.*
YORK. Against them both, my true joints bended be.   [*Kneels.*
  Ill mayst thou thrive, if thou grant any grace !
DUCH. Pleads he in earnest ? Look upon his face ;   100
  His eyes do drop no tears, his prayers are in jest ;
  His words come from his mouth, ours from our breast.
  He prays but faintly and would be denied ;
  We pray with heart and soul, and all beside.
  His weary joints would gladly rise, I know ;   105
  Our knees still kneel till to the ground they grow.
  His prayers are full of false hypocrisy ;
  Ours of true zeal and deep integrity.
  Our prayers do out-pray his ; then let them have
  That mercy which true prayer ought to have.   110
BOLING. Good aunt, stand up.
DUCH.   Nay, do not say ' stand up '.
  Say ' pardon ' first, and afterwards ' stand up '.
  An if I were thy nurse, thy tongue to teach,
  ' Pardon ' should be the first word of thy speech.
  I never long'd to hear a word till now ;   115
  Say ' pardon ' King ; let pity teach thee how.
  The word is short, but not so short as sweet ;
  No word like ' pardon ' for kings' mouths so meet.
YORK. Speak it in French, King, say ' pardonne moy '.
DUCH. Dost thou teach pardon pardon to destroy ?   120
  Ah, my sour husband, my hard-hearted lord,
  That sets the word itself against the word !
  Speak ' pardon ' as 'tis current in our land ;
  The chopping French we do not understand.
  Thine eye begins to speak, set thy tongue there ;   125
  Or in thy piteous heart plant thou thine ear,
  That hearing how our plaints and prayers do pierce,
  Pity may move thee ' pardon ' to rehearse.
BOLING. Good aunt, stand up.
DUCH.   I do not sue to stand ;
  Pardon is all the suit I have in hand.   130
BOLING. I pardon him, as God shall pardon me.

DUCH. O happy vantage of a kneeling knee !
  Yet am I sick for fear.   Speak it again.
  Twice saying ' pardon ' doth not pardon twain,
  But makes one pardon strong.
BOLING.   With all my heart   135
  I pardon him.
DUCH.   A god on earth thou art.
BOLING. But for our trusty brother-in-law and the Abbot,
  With all the rest of that consorted crew,
  Destruction straight shall dog them at the heels.
  Good uncle, help to order several powers   140
  To Oxford, or where'er these traitors are.
  They shall not live within this world, I swear,
  But I will have them, if I once know where.
  Uncle, farewell ; and, cousin, adieu ;
  Your mother well hath pray'd, and prove you true.   145
DUCH. Come, my old son ; I pray God make thee new.   [Exeunt.

SCENE IV.   *Windsor Castle.*

Enter SIR PIERCE OF EXTON *and a* Servant.

EXTON. Didst thou not mark the King, what words he spake ?
  ' Have I no friend will rid me of this living fear ? '
  Was it not so ?
SERV.   These were his very words.
EXTON. ' Have I no friend ? ' quoth he.   He spake it twice
  And urg'd it twice together, did he not ?   5
SERV. He did.
EXTON. And, speaking it, he wishtly look'd on me,
  As who should say ' I would thou wert the man
  That would divorce this terror from my heart ' ;
  Meaning the king at Pomfret.   Come, let's go.   10
  I am the King's friend, and will rid his foe.   [Exeunt.

SCENE V.   *Pomfret Castle.   The dungeon of the Castle.*

Enter KING RICHARD.

K. RICH. I have been studying how I may compare
  This prison where I live unto the world
  And, for because the world is populous
  And here is not a creature but myself,
  I cannot do it.   Yet I'll hammer it out.   5
  My brain I'll prove the female to my soul,
  My soul the father ; and these two beget
  A generation of still-breeding thoughts,
  And these same thoughts people this little world,
  In humours like the people of this world,   10
  For no thought is contented.   The better sort,
  As thoughts of things divine, are intermix'd
  With scruples, and do set the word itself
  Against the word,
  As thus : ' Come, little ones ' ; and then again,   15
  ' It is as hard to come as for a camel
  To thread the postern of a small needle's eye '.

SCENE 21
*Interior. Windsor. A
Corridor in the Castle.
Day.*

SCENE 22
*Interior. A Dungeon
in Pomfret Castle.
Night.*

Thoughts tending to ambition, they do plot
Unlikely wonders : how these vain weak nails
May tear a passage through the flinty ribs   20
Of this hard world, my ragged prison walls ;
And, for they cannot, die in their own pride.
Thoughts tending to content flatter themselves
That they are not the first of fortune's slaves,
Nor shall not be the last ; like silly beggars   25
Who, sitting in the stocks, refuge their shame,
That many have and others must sit there ;
And in this thought they find a kind of ease,
Bearing their own misfortunes on the back
Of such as have before endur'd the like.   30
Thus play I in one person many people,
And none contented.   Sometimes am I king ;
Then treasons make me wish myself a beggar,
And so I am.   Then crushing penury
Persuades me I was better when a king ;   35
Then am I king'd again ; and by and by
Think that I am unking'd by Bolingbroke,
And straight am nothing.   But whate'er I be,
Nor I, nor any man that but man is,
With nothing shall be pleas'd till he be eas'd   40
With being nothing.

                    The music plays.

                Music do I hear ?
Ha, ha ! keep time.   How sour sweet music is
When time is broke and no proportion kept !
So is it in the music of men's lives.
And here have I the daintiness of ear   45
To check time broke in a disorder'd string ;
But, for the concord of my state and time,
Had not an ear to hear my true time broke.
I wasted time, and now doth time waste me ;
For now hath time made me his numb'ring clock :   50
My thoughts are minutes ; and with sighs they jar
Their watches on unto mine eyes, the outward watch,
Whereto my finger, like a dial's point,
Is pointing still, in cleansing them from tears.
Now sir, the sound that tells what hour it is   55
Are clamorous groans which strike upon my heart,
Which is the bell.   So sighs, and tears, and groans,
Show minutes, times, and hours ; but my time
Runs posting on in Bolingbroke's proud joy,
While I stand fooling here, his Jack of the clock.   60
This music mads me.   Let it sound no more ;
For though it have holp madmen to their wits,
In me it seems it will make wise men mad.
Yet blessing on his heart that gives it me !
For 'tis a sign of love ; and love to Richard   65
Is a strange brooch in this all-hating world.

                Enter a Groom *of the stable.*

GROOM. Hail, royal Prince !
K. RICH.   Thanks, noble peer !
  The cheapest of us is ten groats too dear.
  What art thou ? and how comest thou hither,
  Where no man never comes but that sad dog   70
  That brings me food to make misfortune live ?
GROOM. I was a poor groom of thy stable, King,
  When thou wert king ; who, travelling towards York,
  With much ado at length have gotten leave
  To look upon my sometimes royal master's face.   75
  O, how it ern'd my heart, when I beheld,
  In London streets, that coronation-day,
  When Bolingbroke rode on roan Barbary—
  That horse that thou so often hast bestrid,
  That horse that I so carefully have dress'd !   80
K. RICH. Rode he on Barbary ?   Tell me, gentle friend,
  How went he under him ?
GROOM. So proudly as if he disdain'd the ground.
K. RICH. So proud that Bolingbroke was on his back !
  That jade hath eat-bread from my royal hand ;   85
  This hand hath made him proud with clapping him.
  Would he not stumble ? would he not fall down,
  Since pride must have a fall, and break the neck
  Of that proud man that did usurp his back ?
  Forgiveness, horse !   Why do I rail on thee,   90
  Since thou, created to be aw'd by man,
  Wast born to bear ?   I was not made a horse ;
  And yet I bear a burden like an ass,
  Spurr'd, gall'd, and tir'd, by jauncing Bolingbroke.

              Enter Keeper *with meat.*

KEEP. Fellow, give place ; here is no longer stay.   95
K. RICH. If thou love me, 'tis time thou wert away.
GROOM. What my tongue dares not, that my heart shall say. *[Exit.*
KEEP. My lord, will't please you to fall to ?
K. RICH. Taste of it first as thou art wont to do.
KEEP. My lord, I dare not.   Sir Pierce of Exton,
  Who lately came from the King, commands the contrary. 101
K. RICH. The devil take Henry of Lancaster and thee !
  Patience is stale, and I am weary of it.   *[Beats the* Keeper.
KEEP. Help, help, help !

    The murderers, EXTON *and* Servants, *rush in, armed.*

K. RICH. How now !   What means death in this rude assault ? 105
  Villain, thy own hand yields thy death's instrument.
             [Snatching a weapon and killing one.
  Go thou and fill another room in hell.
             [He kills another, then EXTON *strikes him down.*
  That hand shall burn in never-quenching fire
  That staggers thus my person.   Exton, thy fierce hand
  Hath with the King's blood stain'd the King's own land. 110
  Mount, mount, my soul ! thy seat is up on high ;
  Whilst my gross flesh sinks downward, here to die. *[Dies.*
| EXTON. As full of valour as of royal blood. | Lines 113–118
                                                  omitted.

Both have I spill'd.   O, would the deed were good!
For now the devil, that told me I did well,   115
Says that this deed is chronicled in hell.
This dead king to the living king I'll bear.
Take hence the rest, and give them burial here.   [*Exeunt.*

Lines 113–118
omitted.

SCENE VI.   *Windsor Castle.*

Flourish.   Enter BOLINGBROKE, *the* DUKE OF YORK, *with other* Lords
and Attendants.

SCENE 23
*Interior. Westminster
Hall. Day.*

BOLING.   Kind uncle York, the latest news we hear
Is that the rebels have consum'd with fire
Our town of Ciceter in Gloucestershire ;
But whether they be ta'en or slain we hear not.

Enter NORTHUMBERLAND.

Welcome, my lord.   What is the news ?   5
NORTH.   First, to thy sacred state wish I all happiness.
The next news is, I have to London sent
The heads of Salisbury, Spencer, Blunt, and Kent.
The manner of their taking may appear
At large discoursed in this paper here.   10
BOLING.   We thank thee, gentle Percy, for thy pains ;
And to thy worth will add right worthy gains.

Lines 5–18 Omitted,
including entries of
Northumberland and
Fitzwater.

Enter FITZWATER.

FITZ.   My lord, I have from Oxford sent to London
The heads of Brocas and Sir Bennet Seely ;
Two of the dangerous consorted traitors   15
That sought at Oxford thy dire overthrow.
BOLING.   Thy pains, Fitzwater, shall not be forgot ;
Right noble is thy merit, well I wot.

Enter PERCY, *with the* BISHOP OF CARLISLE

PERCY.   The grand conspirator, Abbot of Westminster,
With clog of conscience and sour melancholy,   20
Hath yielded up his body to the grave ;
But here is Carlisle living, to abide
Thy kingly doom, and sentence of his pride.
BOLING.   Carlisle, this is your doom :
Choose out some secret place, some reverend room,   25
More than thou hast, and with it joy thy life ;
So as thou liv'st in peace, die free from strife ;
For though mine enemy thou hast ever been,
High sparks of honour in thee have I seen.

Enter EXTON, *with* Attendants, *bearing a coffin.*

EXTON.   Great King, within this coffin I present   30
Thy buried fear.   Herein all breathless lies
The mightiest of thy greatest enemies,
Richard of Bordeaux, by me hither brought.
BOLING.   Exton, I thank thee not ; for thou hast wrought
A deed of slander with thy fatal hand   35
Upon my head and all this famous land.

EXTON. From your own mouth, my lord, did I this deed.
BOLING. They love not poison that do poison need,
    Nor do I thee.   Though I did wish him dead,
    I hate the murderer, love him murdered.   40
    The guilt of conscience take thou for thy labour,
    But neither my good word nor princely favour ;
    With Cain go wander thorough shades of night,
    And never show thy head by day nor light.
    Lords, I protest my soul is full of woe   45
    That blood should sprinkle me to make me grow.
    Come, mourn with me for what I do lament,
    And put on sullen black incontinent.
    I'll make a voyage to the Holy Land,
    To wash this blood off from my guilty hand.   50
    March sadly after ; grace my mournings here
    In weeping after this untimely bier.   *[Exeunt.*

GLOSSARY

Scott Shane

Difficult phrases are listed under the most important or most difficult word in them. If no such word stands out, they are listed under the first word.

Words appear in the form they take in the text. If they occur in several forms, they are listed under the root form (singular for nouns, infinitive for verbs).

Line references are given only when the same word is used with different meanings, and when there are puns.

A GOD'S NAME, in God's name

ABEL, murdered by his brother Cain; *see* Genesis iv

ABRAHAM, 'bosom of good old Abraham', proverbial for 'restful peace of heaven'

ABSENT TIME, time of the absence (of King Richard)

ACCOMPLISH'D WITH, having attained

ACCOUNT, debt

ADVISED, deliberate

AFFECTS, 'banish their affects', take their affections into banishment

AGAINST, in expectation of

AGUE, fever, sickness

ALARMS, troubles, disturbances

ALMSMAN, one who lives on charity

AMAZ'D, bewildered, perplexed

AMAZING, stupefying

AN IF, if

ANCIENT, long-standing

ANSWER, 'days of answer', trial-days

ANTIC, clown, jester

ANTIPODES, people who live on the other side of the earth

APPARENT, obvious

APPEACH, denounce, accuse publicly

APPEAL (v.), accuse; (n.), accusation

APPELLANT (n.), one who accuses, challenger; (adj.), in accusation

APPOINTMENTS, (i) intentions, purposes; (ii) arms and equipment

APPREHENSION, conception

APPROVED, proven, demonstrated

APRICOCKS, apricots

ARGUMENT, subject

AS, in so far as (I iii 55)

ASPECT, look, appearance

AT LARGE, in full

ATONE, reconcile

ATTACH, arrest

ATTAINDER, accusation

AWFUL, filled with awe, reverential

AY, yes (with pun on the pronoun 'I', IV i 201)

AYE, ever

BADGES, emblems

BAFFL'D, publicly disgraced

BAIT, persecute, torment

BALM, consecrated oil used in the coronation of a king

BAND, bond

BARBARY, a breed of horse; here, also the name of a particular horse

BARBED, armoured

BARKLOUGHLY, probably a corrupt form of the equivalent of the modern Harlech, in Wales

BASE COURT, lower or outer courtyard (with pun on 'base', mean, despicable, III iii 180, 182)

BAY, hunted animal's last stand

BEADS, prayer-beads; 'set of beads', rosary

BEADSMEN, pensioners who offer prayers for their benefactors

BEGGAR AND THE KING, THE, the name of an old ballad

BEGUILE, (i) pleasantly divert attention from (II iii 11); (ii) deceive (IV i 281)

BELIKE, probably

BENEVOLENCES, forced loans

BESHREW, confound, curse

BETID, happened

BETIMES, soon, early

BIAS, natural curved path followed by the weighted ball in the game of bowls

BILLS, weapons, each consisting of a long staff with a curved blade

BLANK CHARTERS, documents requiring loans to the crown from wealthy persons, the amounts to be filled in by the king's 'substitutes'

BLANKS, see BLANK CHARTERS

BONDSLAVE, 'Thy state of law is bondslave to the law', your legal status is that of a subject who must obey the law, not that of a king

BOON, favour

BOOT (n.), alternative, remedy; (v.), helps, avails

BOUND (n.), (i) bounce, rebound (I ii 58); (ii) limit, confine (V ii 38); (adj.), obligated, in debt

BRANDS, coals

BRAVING, defiant

BREED, ancestral reputation (II i 52)

BRISTOW, Bristol

BRITAINE, Brittany

BROKE, escaped

BROKING PAWN, the possession of the king's moneylenders

BROOCH, 'strange brooch', rare jewel

BROOKS, enjoys

BURY MINE INTENTS, conceal my plans

BY, nearby (IV i 123)

CAIN, murderer of his brother Abel; see Genesis iv

CAITIFF, (i) wretched; (ii) captive

CARE, (i) responsibility; (ii) diligence; (iii) grief; (iv) anxiety (elaborate puns involving all of these meanings, IV i 195–8)

CAREER, charge (in tournament or battle)

CAREFUL BUSINESS, anxious preoccupation

CARVER, 'Be his own carver', help himself (suggesting both table-knife and sword)

CASQUE, helmet

CATERPILLARS, parasites, devourers

CHALLENGE LAW, demand legal rights

CHANGE, exchange

CHARGE, expense, outlay

CHECK, rebuke

CHEERLY, cheerily

CHOLER, anger

CHOPPING, changing in meaning

CICETER, Cirencester

CIVIL, of or between the citizens of one nation (cf. 'civil war')

CLAPPING, patting

CLEAN, completely, utterly

CLERK, assistant who uttered responses (e.g. 'amen') to the priest's prayers

CLIMATE, CLIME, place, region

CLOG, burden

CLOGGING, heavy, burdensome, awkward

COAT, 'household coat', coat of arms

COMFORTABLE, comforting

COMMEND (v.), commit, hand over

COMMENDS (n.), greetings

COMPASSIONATE, (i) sorrowfully lamenting; (ii) appealing for pity

COMPLOT, conspire

COMPOSITION, constitution, condition

CONCEIT, fantasy, fanciful imagination

CONCLUDE, come to terms

CONDITION, personal quality, trait

CONDUCT, escort

CONFOUND, destroy

CONJURATION, 'senseless conjuration', entreaty addressed to senseless things

CONSEQUENTLY, subsequently

CONSORTED, conspiring

CONVEY, (i) conduct (IV i 316); (ii) steal (IV i 317)

CONVEYERS, thieves

CORMORANT, glutton

COURSER, swift horse

COUSIN, relative

COVER YOUR HEADS, replace your hats (which have been removed as a sign of respect)

COZENING, cheating

CRAVE, demand, desire

CREST-FALLEN, humiliated

CROSSES, thwartings, troubles

CROSSLY, adversely

CROWNS, heads (III iii 96)

CRYSTAL, clear, bright
CUNNING, skilfully made
CURRENT, valid

DASTARD, coward
DATELESS LIMIT, limitless term
DEAD TIME, (i) past time; (ii) fatal time (pun, IV i 10)
DEAR, (i) of great value (I i 130, I iii 156, II i 57–8); (ii) grievous, bitter (I iii 151)
DEARTH, famine
DECEIVABLE, deceptive
DEFEND, 'God defend', God forbid
DENY, refuse
DEPOSE, examine under oath
DEPRESS'D, brought low, humbled
DESIGN, point out (by giving victory to)
DESPITE OF, in spite of
DETERMINATE, bring to an end
DIGRESSING, transgressing
DISCOMFORTABLE, discouraging
DISPARK'D, opened game parks to other uses
DISPATCH, (i) execute (III i 35); (ii) hurry (IV i 243)
DISPOSE OF, make arrangements for
DISTAFF-WOMEN, spinning women
DISTRAIN'D, seized
DIVINE, prophesy
DOOM, judgement
DOUBLE, forked
DOUBLE-FATAL YEW, bearing poisonous berries and furnishing wood for bows
DOUBT, ''tis doubt', it is feared
DRAYMEN, cart-drivers
DRESS'D, groomed
DUGS, breasts
DUST, speck of dust

EAGER, sharp
EAR, plough, cultivate
EAT, eaten
EFFEMINATE, self-indulgent
ELECT, ELECTED, chosen
EMBASSAGE, message
ENDOWMENTS, possessions, wealth
ENFRANCHISEMENT, (i) liberation (I iii 90); (ii) freedom from banishment, restoration of rights (III iii 114)
ENGAOL'D, imprisoned
ENJOY, possess; 'to enjoy', in the hope of possessing

ENSIGN, flag
ENTREATED, treated
ENVY, malice, hatred
ERN'D, grieved
ESPY, observe, see
ESTEEM, account, consider
ESTIMATE, reputation
EXACTLY, explicitly
EXCLAIMS, outcries
EXPEDIENCE, speed
EXPEDIENT, speedy
EXTINCT, extinguished
EYE OF HEAVEN, sun

FAC'D, countenanced
FACTION TRAITORS, 'revolted faction traitors', rebellious band of traitors
FAINT, grow faint-hearted
FAINTLY, faint-heartedly
FALL, shed, let fall
FALL TO, begin (eating)
FANTASTIC, existing only in imagination
FARM, lease the right of taxing, in return for a fixed cash payment
FAVOURS, (i) faces, appearances; (ii) benefits, friendly acts (pun, IV i 168)
FEALTY, loyalty
FEARFUL, frightened
FELL, cruel
FELLOW, equal
FIGUR'D, embossed, decorated
FIGURE, image
FIRST, 'on the first', of the former kind
FLATTER WITH, try to please
FOIL, metal leaf placed under a gem to give additional brilliance
FOND, (i) foolish (V i 101); (ii) tender, affectionate (pun on (i) and (ii), V ii 95, V ii 101)
FONDLY, (i) foolishly (III iii 185, IV i 72); (ii) affectionately, lovingly (III ii 9)
FONT, baptismal font
FOR, as (II iii 114)
FOR THAT, because
FOR WHY, because of which
FORFEND, forbid
FORWARD, willing
FRETTED, worn down
FROZEN, (i) cold in manner; (ii) caused by chill which produced ague (pun, II i 117)

GAGE, token of defiance, probably a glove

'GAINST, in preparation for

GALL'D, made sore

GLASS, mirror

GLENDOWER, famous Welsh soldier, possibly the 'Welsh Captain' in II iv

GLIST'RING, shining, glittering

GLOSE, speak flatteringly

GNARLING, snarling

GOD FOR HIS MERCY, may God show mercy

GOLGOTHA, hill where Christ was crucified; literally, 'place of skulls'

GOOD, high in rank (I i 40)

GRACE, dignify with one's presence

GREAT, swollen with grief (II i 228)

GRIPE, grasp, clutch

GROAT, a coin worth four pence; 'ten groats', the difference in value between a 'royal' and a 'noble', both coins

HALLOA'D, hollered, shouted

HALLOWMAS, 1 November, All Saints' Day

HAP, fortune

HAPPILY, (i) happily; (ii) perhaps

HAPPY, fortunate

HARD-FAVOUR'D, ugly

HARDLY, with difficulty

HAUGHT, haughty

HAVIOUR, behaviour

HEAD, source; 'taking so the head', (i) thus omitting the title; (ii) thus acting without restraint (pun, III iii 14)

HEIGHT, high rank

HEIR, offspring

HIE, go

HIGH-STOMACH'D, haughty

HOLLOW, insincere

HOLP, helped

HOMAGE, pledge of loyalty

HOUSEHOLD COAT, coat of arms

HUMOURS, peculiar characters, temperaments

IDLY, (i) foolishly (III iii 171); (ii) listlessly (V ii 25)

ILL LEFT, (i) left badly equipped; (ii) left in disorder

ILL-ERECTED, built with evil results

IMAGERY, 'painted imagery', painted cloths depicting speaking figures, often hung in Elizabethan houses

IMP OUT, repair by grafting new feathers on

IMPEACH, discredit, call into question

IMPRESE, heraldic emblem

INCONTINENT, immediately

INDIFFERENT, impartial

INFECTION, moral or physical contamination

INHABITABLE, not habitable

INHERIT US, put us in possession of

INSINUATE, act ingratiatingly, wheedle oneself into favour

INTERCHANGEABLY, in turn

INTERCHANGEABLY SET DOWN THEIR HANDS, signed reciprocally (each retaining a copy with the others' signatures as well as his own)

ISSUE, descendants

JACK OF THE CLOCK, small figure of a man which strikes the hours

JADE, poor horse

JAR, tick

JAUNCING, prancing (or causing a horse to prance)

JEST, play a part in a masque or play

JOURNEYMAN, (i) qualified craftsman who serves a master craftsman for day-wages; (ii) traveller (pun, I iii 274)

JOY, gladden, enjoy

JUSTS, jousts, tournaments

KERNS, light-armed Irish foot soldiers

KIND, (i) manner, fashion (II iii 143, 146); (ii) fellow-countrymen (IV i 141)

KNOTS, flower-beds laid out in intricate patterns

LARGE, 'at large', in full

LARGESS, expenditure on gifts

LATE, recent, recently

LEAN-LOOK'D, lean-looking

LEARN, teach

LEAVE, leave off, stop

LENDINGS, money advanced to soldiers when regular pay cannot be given

LETTERS PATENTS, letters from the king conferring a right or privilege

LEWD, base, improper

LIBERAL, unrestrained, free

LIE IN, depends upon

LIEF, 'as lief', as gladly

LIGHT, dismount

LIGHTENS FORTH, flashes

LIMITS, banks
LINEAL ROYALTIES, hereditary rights
LINGERS, causes to linger
LINING, contents
LIST (v.), listen to
LISTS (n.), tournament-ground
LIVERY, 'sue . . . livery', obtain by legal suit the possession of an inheritance
LODGE, beat down
LODGINGS, rooms
LOOK WHAT, whatever
LOOK'D WHEN, expected that
LOUR, threaten, scowl
LOWER WORLD, other side of the world

MAIM, crippling injury
MAKE, do (V iii 89)
MAKE A LEG, submissively bend the knee
MANAGE, management, control
MANNER, 'in manner', so to speak
MANUAL SEAL OF DEATH, (i) death warrant bearing the authoritative seal; (ii) the gage (glove), since it is 'manual', i.e. of the hand (pun, IV i 25)
MAP, image, epitome
MARRY, indeed
MARS, the god of war
MATCH, game
MEAN, low-born
MEASURE (n.), (i) a stately dance (I iii 291); (ii) moderation (pun on (i) and (ii), III iv 7–8); (v.), travel across
MERELY, purely
MERIT, reward
METRES, verses
METTLE, essence, substance
MISCREANT, heretical villain
MISTAKE, (i) misunderstand, take amiss (II ii 74, III iii 15); (ii) transgress, take what is not yours (III iii 17)
MODEL, (i) image (I ii 28); (ii) microcosm (III ii 153, III iv 42); (iii) ground plan of a ruin (V i 11)
MOE, more
MONARCHIZE, play monarch
MORE, again
MORTAL, fatal, deadly
MORTAL TIMES, the lives of mortal men
MOTIVE, moving part; i.e., tongue (I i 193)

NAKED, undefended

NAME, title
NEAR, 'be ne'er the near', and still be no nearer (to each other)
NEPTUNE, god of the sea
NEUTER, neutral
NEW WORLD, world under a new king (IV i 78)
NEW WORLD'S CROWN, heavenly crown (V i 24)
NICELY, (i) subtly, elegantly; (ii) trivially, triflingly (pun, II i 84)
NOBLE, (i) coin worth six shillings and eight pence (I i 88); (ii) of noble birth (pun on (i) and (ii), V v 67)
NOBLESSE, nobility
NOISOME, harmful, dangerous
NOTE, mark of disgrace
NUMB'RING CLOCK, clock showing hours and minutes (as opposed to hourglass)

OBJECT, bring as a charge
OFFICE, (i) workroom (I ii 69); (ii) service (II ii 137)
OPPRESSION, burden
OR, either
OSTENTATION, display
OUTDAR'D, (i) surpassed in daring; (ii) dared down, intimidated
OVER-BLOWN, blown over, passed
OWES, owns

PAINTED IMAGERY, painted cloths depicting speaking figures, often hung in Elizabethan houses
PALE, fence, fenced area
PALMER, pilgrim
PALSY, paralysis
PARDONNE MOY, excuse me (and thus a polite way of refusing a request)
PARLE, PARLEY, trumpet-call to a meeting to discuss the terms of a truce
PART, part from
PARTIAL SLANDER, accusation of partiality
PARTIALIZE, make partial
PARTY, 'upon his party', on his side; 'on thy royal party', on your part
PARTY-VERDICT, contribution to the joint verdict
PASSAGES, experiences
PASSENGERS, travellers
PASTE, pastry cover to a meat pie

PELICAN, believed to feed its young with its own blood

PELTING, paltry

PENURY, poverty, destitution

PERFORCE, (i) by force (II iii 121); (ii) of necessity (V ii 35)

PERSPECTIVES, pictures designed to be intelligible only when viewed from the side

PESTILENCE, plague

PHAETHON, drove the sun-chariot of Apollo, his father, too close to earth, and was killed by Zeus' thunderbolt

PIECE THE WAY OUT, make the distance seem longer

PILL'D, plundered

PINES THE CLIME, afflicts the land

PINS, 'a row of pins', i.e. a very trivial thing (in a wager)

PITCH, peak of a falcon's flight

PITIFUL, compassionate, full of pity

PLACE, 'give place', go away

PLAINING, complaining

PLANTED, established

PLASHY, Gloucester's country estate in Essex

PLATED, dressed in armour

PLUME-PLUCK'D, humbled

POINT, 'dial's point', hand of a clock

POLICY, political wisdom

POMFRET, Pontefract Castle, in Yorkshire

POMPOUS, splendid

POORLY, humbly, abjectly

PORTCULLIS'D, enclosed, fortified

POSSESS'D, (i) put in possession (II i 107); (ii) mad, possessed by a devil (II i 108)

POST, ride with great speed; 'in post', in haste; 'spur post', ride in haste

POSTE-HASTE, with all possible speed

POSTERN, small gate or door

POWER, army

PRECEDENT, proof

PRESAGES, omens, forebodings

PRESENCE, royal reception-room

PRESENTLY, immediately

PRESS'D, drafted, conscripted

PRESS'D TO DEATH, crushed to death by heavy weights (the punishment for a felon who refused to speak)

PREVENT, avoid

PRICK, urge, provoke

PRIDE, (i) pride; (ii) prime, best condition (pun, V v 22)

PRIVATE WRONGS, the wrongs suffered by private citizens

PRODIGAL, excessive, extravagant (with a suggestion of the Biblical 'prodigal son')

PRODIGY, monstrous birth

PROFANE, (i) misuse (I iii 59, I iv 13); (ii) commit sacrilege (III iii 81)

PROOF, invulnerability

PROPERTY, distinctive quality

PROPORTION, musical rhythm

PROPORTIONABLE, in a reasonable proportion

PURCHASE, acquire

QUIT THEIR GRIEFS, requite their sad tales

RAG'D (v.), enraged

RAGE (n.), violence

RAGGED, rugged

RANKLE, cause a festering wound

RASH, rapid

RAVEL OUT, unravel

RAVENSPURGH, a port on the River Humber

RAW, inexperienced

RAZE, erase, obliterate

REAR, raise to life (by saving from execution)

REBUKES, 'Gaunt's rebukes', the insults suffered by Gaunt

RECEIPT, sum of money received

RECREANT (n.), (i) coward; (ii) traitor; (adj.), (i) cowardly; (ii) disloyal

REDOUBTED, dread, feared

REFIN'D, civilised

REFUGE, find refuge from

REGARD, 'wit's regard', the thoughtful consideration of reason

REGENT, ruler

REGREET, (i) salute, greet (I iii 67); (ii) greet again (I iii 142, 168)

REHEARSE, repeat, pronounce

REMAIN, dwell

REMEDIES, 'want their remedies', cannot cure what gives rise to them

REMEMBER, remind

REPAIR, go, return

REPEALS, calls back from exile

RESPECT, 'there's no respect', no one cares

RESPECT'ST NOT, do not hesitate to

RETIR'D, withdrawn

RETURN, answer, reply

REVEREND ROOM, place of religious retirement
REVERSION, legal succession, inheritance
REVOLTED FACTION TRAITORS, rebellious band of traitors
RHEUM, watery discharge, tears
RID, get rid of
ROAN, of mixed colour (said of a horse)
ROOM, place (V v 107)
ROUNDLY, bluntly
ROUSE, startle (an animal) from its lair
ROYAL, (i) royal; (ii) a coin worth ten shillings (pun, V v 67)
ROYALTIES, rights granted by the king
RUBS, obstacles in the game of bowls which divert the ball from its natural course
RUE, herb associated with grace
RUG-HEADED, shaggy-haired
RUTH, pity

SCOPE, (i) aim, object (III iii 112); (ii) opportunity, permission (III iii 140), (pun on (i) and (ii), III iii 141)
SCRUPLES, doubts
SEAL, wax seal hanging from a document; 'manual seal', see MANUAL
SEAT, throne
SECURE, over-confident
SECURELY, (i) confidently (I iii 97); (ii) over-confidently (II i 266)
SECURITY, over-confidence
SELF, same
SELF-BORNE, initiated by, and carried for, one's own amibition
SETS, puts up a stake against, challenges
SEVERAL, various
SHADOW, (i) delusive semblance (II ii 14, 23); (ii) external display (IV i 292, 294, 297); (iii) image, reflection (IV i 293)
SHEER, pure
SHIVERS, splinters, fragments
SHORT'ST OF DAY, 22 December, the winter solstice
SHREWD, harmful, malicious
SIFT, determine by questioning
SIGNORIES, estates
SILLY, simple-minded
SIX AND SEVEN, 'at six and seven', in confusion
SLUIC'D OUT, caused to flow out
SLY, stealthy

SMALL AND SMALL, little by little
SMOOTH, gloss over
SOMETIMES, sometime, former
SOMEWHAT, something
SOOTH, flattery
SORT, group, pack
SOUNDED, inquired of
SOUR, bitter
SPOTTED, stained with sin
SPRIGHTFULLY, spiritedly
SPUR POST, ride in haste
STAGGERS, causes to stagger
STAND OUT, resist
STANDS UPON YOUR GRACE, is up to you
STARS, 'fair stars', noble birth
STATE, politics (III iv 27)
STAY, wait
STERLING, valid currency
STEWS, brothels
STILL, always, continually
STOOPING DUTY, submissive kneeling
STRAIGHT, immediately
STRANGER, foreign
STREAMING, flying
STREW'D, covered with rushes
STRIKE, (i) strike sail, lower sail; (ii) resist, strike back (pun, II i 266)
STUBBORN JEWRY, the land of the Jews, both (i) rough, barbarous; and (ii) obstinate (in resisting Christianity)
SUBJECTED, (i) made a subject; (ii) subjected to ordinary needs and troubles (pun, III ii 176)
SUBSCRIBE THEM, put their names down
SUE LIVERY, obtain by legal suit the possession of an inheritance
SUFFER, allow, permit
SUGGEST, tempt, incite
SULLEN, melancholy
SULLENS, sulks
SURETIES, men responsible for the appearance of defendants at their trials
SURFEIT, excess, overindulgence
SYMPATHIZE, respond to
SYMPATHY, correspondence, equality (of rank)

TAPER, candle
TEEMING DATE, period of childbearing
TEMPER, quality, excellence (of a sword)

TEND, (i) refer (II i 232); (ii) go along with, attend on (IV i 199)

TENDER, (i) care about (I i 32); (ii) offer (II iii 41)

TENEMENT, rented building or land

TESTAMENT, will

THOROUGH, through

THRIVE, 'to thrive', help me to thrive (I iii 84); 'thrives to', succeeds in (II ii 144)

THROW, (i) throw down glove as gage; (ii) throw dice (pun, IV i 57)

TIED, required

TIMELESS, untimely

TIMES, 'minutes, times, and hours', quarter-hours and half-hours

TOILED, exhausted

TORN, broken

TOTTERED, tattered, dilapidated

TRADE, traffic, passage

TREASON, 'speak treason', i.e. call the king a fool

TRIUMPHS, celebrations

TROW, believe

TRY, put to the test

UNAVOIDED, unavoidable

UNDERBEARING, enduring

UNDO, (i) undress; (ii) ruin, destroy (pun, IV i 203)

UNFELT, intangible, not accompanied by proof

UNGRACIOUS, wicked, profane

UNKINDNESS, (i) unkindness; (ii) unnatural behaviour

UNSTAID, unrestrained

UNTHRIFTS, spendthrifts

UNTHRIFTY, spendthrift

UNTRUTH, disloyalty

URGE, emphasise, insist on (III i 4, V iv 5)

VANTAGE, profit, gain

VASSAL, subject

VENGE, avenge

VENOM, snakes' poison (alluding to the legend that St Patrick had rid Ireland of snakes) (II i 157)

VERGE, compass, circumference

WAIL, 'ways to wail', paths to grief

WANT, lack

WANTON, (i) luxuriant (I iii 214); (ii) spoiled, pampered (V iii 10); 'make woe wanton', (i) make a game of woe; (ii) make woe unrestrained or pampered (pun, V, i 101)

WANTONS, 'play the wantons', trifle, play a game

WARDER, staff used as a signal by one presiding over a formal combat

WASTE, destruction of a landlord's property by a tenant (II i 103)

WATCH (n.), night watchmen (V iii 9); 'outward watch', clock face; (v.), stay awake at night

WATCHES, 'jar Their watches', tick their intervals of time

WELL-GRAC'D, (i) graceful; (ii) well-received, popular (pun, V ii 24)

WHENCESOEVER, from somewhere or other

WHERE, whereas (III ii 185)

WHEREWITHAL, by means of which

WHILE, until (I iii 122)

WHITE-BEARDS, old men

WILL, desire, natural inclination

WINDOWS' TOPS, upper windows

WINK, shut one's eyes

WISHTLY, intently and longingly

WITHAL, (i) nonetheless (II i 188); (ii) besides (IV i 18)

WITHOUT, outside (V ii 56)

WITNESSING, foretelling, betokening

WIT'S REGARD, the thoughtful consideration of reason

WONT, accustomed

WORD, 'the word itself Against the word', one passage of Scripture against another

WORST, most unfit by reason of rank (IV i 115)

WORTHILY, deservedly, justly

WORTHY, deserved

WOT, know

WRINKLE, frown

WROUGHT IT WITH, persuaded, or collaborated with

ZEAL, loyalty